Portrait In Progress

How to See
Yourself as a Masterpiece
in the Making

Portrait In Progress

How to See
Yourself as a Masterpiece
in the Making

By Dr. Ken Nichols

ISBN #09675098-0-7

Published by ALIVE Ministries
(619) 590-1747
www.alive@shadowmountain.com

Dedication

This book is dedicated to our three precious children - Mark Alan, Kendra Kay and Kara Lynn. God has graciously blessed us, and we are eternally grateful.

Parenting is such an important influence in the fashioning of a healthy self-concept.
Marlene and I dedicated ourselves to build into our children the qualities of character, spiritual value and personal traits that would prepare them for the challenges of life. And sometimes unknowingly, our good intentions and worthy goals were the very things that bruised their self-esteem.

One of the great joys of parenting is to watch the gradual maturing process in your children. Each of our children has followed a unique path. Each has a unique personality. They are at different places in their journey toward personal and spiritual maturity. They each have abundant evidence that the Master Artist has touched-up our imperfect parenting and is fashioning them into His image.

Mark is disciplined in his life. He has unquestioning integrity and has achieved good success in his law-enforcement career. He loves his wife and children and is a faithful friend. He has a commitment to excellence in whatever he pursues in life.

Kendra has a very special gift of encouragement. Her joy for life is contagious. She has a delightful sense of humor. Her selfless love and servant's heart is evident in her marriage and family. She is a loving and loyal friend.

Kara is a genuinely sensitive person. She has a laser-sharp sensitivity to people who have special needs. She is a discerning counselor and faithful encourager to friends who are down and discouraged. She is very creative, loves art and music, and is developing good writing skills.

All three of our children know Christ as Savior. God is at work in their lives in very special ways. Whatever human limitations they may have are only opportunities for the Master Artist to make brush marks of eternal value on their Portrait in Progress.

Ken & Marlene Nichols
Grateful Parents

Books and Resources
By Dr. Ken Nichols

Reading Resources:

- *Harnessing the Incredible Power of Fear*
- *Fear Book Study Guide*
- *El Temor*
- *Prescription for a Healthy Heart*
- *Healing Freedom of Forgiveness*
- *Overcoming the Overwhelming*
- *Maximizing Marriage*

Seminar Tapes:

- Age-Old Truth/New Age Times
- Managing Burdens
- Principles for Partnership
- Personal Contentment
- Portrait of a Person
- Strength for Spiritual Warfare
- Healthy Relationships
- Harnessing Power of Fear
- Prescription for a Healthy Heart
- Pride and Anger
- Purposeful Living

CONTENTS

Special Recognition

This project was truly a team effort. Thank God for those who have so faithfully provided financial assistance, time, and talent. Carol Lacey, a faithful and gifted writing partner, took the rough draft of the material and brought it into focus. Rebecca Calvert, a professor at Christian Heritage College, invested hours in reading, writing, and editing the manuscript. Marlene, my faithful partner in marriage and ministry added many good insights and suggestions. My children provided valuable feedback and important insights that were included in the final copy. Bev Sewell critiqued the final draft and made dozens of practical suggestions that enhanced the overall quality of the book.

Introduction

PORTRAIT IN PROGRESS

Over the past thirty years I have had the great privilege of working with young people. I served for many years as a Youth Pastor and can still remember the turbulence that many teens faced. Their effort to deal with how they viewed themselves, especially in comparison with others, was a never-ending struggle. Some developed rather healthy ways of compensating for a sagging self-esteem: achievement, personal discipline, and commitment to excellence. Others would hurt themselves with destructive responses like promiscuity, alcohol, drugs, or compulsive behaviors.

Although a little more sophisticated, college students are constantly monitoring how they are measuring up to what others expect of them. During my lengthy career as a college professor and administrator, I have counseled with students who were literally experiencing a form of emotional and relational paralysis because of a sagging self-esteem.

In today's headlines, people across America are asking, what has happened to our children? Why do teens shoot and kill others with no regret? What motivates teens to ruin their lives with destructive habits? Is there any explanation for the skyrocketing suicide rates?

But the struggle to find a trusted way of viewing self is not unique to children and teens. Adults at every age also experience a crescendo of personal, emotional, and relational liabilities related to the agonizing absence of a clear and consistent way of seeing self.

People of all ages experience an overwhelming sense of futility in trying to measure up to the ever-changing and always escalating standard of self-worth.

In some ways it is difficult to explain the incredible freedom that results from being able to see yourself from an internal and eternal perspective. The transformation from an exclusively extrinsic (outward) way of measuring self-worth to an intrinsic (inward) perspective is a critical turning point that will last a lifetime.

In our effort to grasp a clear picture of our inner struggle we tighten our grip around an idea that helps us understand many of our inner doubts and fears about self–a metaphor or simile for example: "Life is not a drama, it is drama"; Erma Bombeck wrote a book entitled *If Life is a Bowl of Cherries, What am I Doing in the Pits?* Christians make the same comparisons: God is my co-pilot; God is my anchor; He is the Potter, I am the clay.

Each of these provides a way of viewing ourselves in relationship with the Creator God. But no metaphor captures the essence of our life journey more than seeing ourselves as a masterpiece in the making. It is this biblical concept that helps us cooperate with the Master Artist in the re-creating process of a lifetime. He chooses the model, determines the setting, builds the foundation, creates the colorful palette, deciphers each intricate detail, and skillfully completes His perfect workmanship.

> "For we are His workmanship, created in Christ Jesus for good works, which God prepared beforehand that we should walk in them." (Ephesians 2:10)

The core purpose of this book is to identify and understand the many discouraging voices inside us and around us that create self-conscious doubts about how we see ourselves and how others see us. It is to declare boldly that we can ultimately become the masterpiece we are meant to be if we listen to His teaching, follow His instruction, and cooperate with His workmanship.

Mona Hsu is the Librarian at Christian Heritage College. She is a faithful and capable servant with many God-given talents. She wrote this poem to express the core concept of this book:

Portrait In Progress

Each color of joy and fun
Each line of peace and pain
Are all God's perfect plan
Through our Master's skillful hand.
Stroke by stroke, line by line
He molds us slowly according to His design.
At times...
He seemingly stopped and left me aside
Impatiently I waited and sighed.
He must have forgotten his portrait, I cried.
At times...
He quickly added one line after another.
What was in His mind, I wondered
Shall I be lovely, shall I be wonderful
Softly He whispered
"In my time,
I will finish your portrait with the image
of my beloved son, Jesus Christ."

THE PREPARATION

Identifying the Distractions

As I grew up, I was not aware of the importance of how I viewed myself. As most young children and teens do, I experienced feelings of inadequacies and struggled with self-conscious insecurities. It seemed I was always wondering whether I was doing a good job. Parents, peers, pastors, teachers, and coaches had performance expectations. And for most people early in life the perceived or real expectations of others become the measuring stick of their self-worth. It is not at all unusual to have doubts about measuring up. The expectations of others became a major source of motivation for me. Not everyone responds that way. Some are overwhelmed and discouraged and do all they can to protect their inability to meet the mark.

As for me, I used humor and downright orneriness to cover my self-doubts. I was much more interested in having fun than in paying attention in class. Some teachers knew just how to get the most out of me. Others made me their special project or their target for criticism.

From our earliest memories we have learned to value ourselves through what significant others say of us. Feedback from others to a large extent formed our own self-image. If we received "good grades" from others we thought of ourselves as good. If others treated us poorly or constantly reminded us of our weaknesses we thought of ourselves as not meeting the mark and not worthy of love and affirmation. One of my good friends stated that his mother would constantly say, "You'll never amount to a hill of beans." It wasn't until after I became a Christian that I began to get a glimpse of how God saw me. Sometimes I was flattered with His love, and sometimes I was embarrassed because I disappointed Him. I was too immature to truly understand the concept of becoming a Masterpiece in the Making. I knew in my heart I wanted to please my Heavenly Father and that He was working to grow me spiritually.

As much as we might be encouraged by the concept of becoming a masterpiece, we are all too familiar with our personal and spiritual blemishes.

Until the truth of what God's Word says about who we are and what we are becoming works its way into our reality, our self-image is dominated by the need for self-protection. Our fears motivate us to master the art of projecting acceptable images. And sadly, the more preoccupied we become with self, the less we are able to freely cooperate with God's work in our lives. Our response to a negative view of self seems paradoxical. On the one hand we seem driven to compensate, and on the other hand we are motivated to cooperate with the Master Artist.

———————————————— ◆ ————————————————

Compensating for self-conscious doubts is natural – cooperating with the Master Artist is supernatural.

———————————————— ◆ ————————————————

As the image-bearers of the Lord Jesus Christ, we have been, and are continually being, seriously damaged by Satan and sin. This master of deceit and the father of lies fuels the endless obsession of trying to compensate for our sin-caused blemishes.

There are many personal and spiritual blemishes that will distract you from seeing yourself as a masterpiece in the making. Use your imagination to view yourself as an artist in training and a portrait in progress. See if you can identify with the many voices within, negative distractions and unkind critics. Throughout this book we will filter the content through our "art student" metaphor. Imagine that you are a student (as you are), responding to the teaching and leading of your Master Artist as He directs you through your Portrait in Progress.

2

INTIMIDATION

The student confidently set up her easel, opened her paint box, placed her white gessoed canvas in place, stood her brushes in a jar, clipped the snapshot to the top of the easel, took out her sketch pencil, and stood back to eyeball the image she was about to paint. It was a three-by-five picture of her, taken when her hair looked nice, her eyes sparkled, and her smile was radiant. A snapshot taken outside, sunshine good, shadows obvious, a subtle background. A fine photo. Maybe not much character showing through yet. But when the oil painting was finished, it would express in summary form the fullness of who she was. It would reveal how well she had followed the patient and persistent instructions of the master teacher.

With a burst of enthusiasm she began the tedious process of communicating through the canvas how she saw herself. Her confidence and enthusiasm were short-lived. Voices within and critics all around quickly distorted the image she wanted so badly to portray on the canvas.

Before placing pencil to canvas she glanced around the outdoor classroom at the other students and seasoned artists adjusting their easels, beginning to sketch whatever subject they had selected, choosing their paints, intent on their own progress. The professor walked around helping his students, turning easels to get the best light, answering questions. People passing by stopped to see what was going on. Not much to see, yet. The artists were just beginning.

The girl turned back to her canvas and began to mark proportion points. She recalled the professor's instructions: "Start with three reference points: the distance from the highest place on the forehead where the hairline begins down to the top of the eyebrows, the distance from the top of the eyebrows to the bottom of the nose, and the distance from the bottom of the nose to the bottom of the chin." Quickly and deftly she began to sketch a likeness of her photo.

Criticism. One of the other students looked over her shoulder. "Is that the best photo you could find? It's a little washed out." He turned back to his easel, not noticing that the girl hesitated, pencil in hand. *Well, I still think I can get a good painting out of it,* she thought. Soon she had a good workable sketch and began to squeeze out the oils onto the palette: titanium white, yellow ochre, venetian red, raw umber.

Unfortunately, most of us have plenty of critics who would easily discourage us and keep us from hearing the "still small voice" of God's faithful encouragement. It is easy to forget encouraging and complimentary words. We seem to rehearse and remember the criticisms.

Confusion. "Why didn't you choose watercolor? I think watercolor is much more feminine than oils." A passerby voiced his opinion. She smiled at him briefly and turned back to her canvas, suffering feelings of self-doubt. *Maybe oil is a little too strong. But I've started now; might as well make the best of it.* Quickly she began to slather a background with a diluted mixture, remembering that she had to add to the paint "two parts turpentine to one part poppy seed oil."

"I hope you're not going to paint that dress you're wearing in the photo. I never liked that color on you." *What in the world is Mom doing here?*

"No, Mom. I'll change the dress." She hadn't really considered making it different, but it was easier to bend than to argue. As her mother wandered off to compare her daughter's painting with the other artists' work, the girl reached for a tube of paint. Then keeping in mind all she had observed, what the many books and teachers had taught her, and her own experimentation, she mixed her colors and began applying paint to the sketch. A lot of light behind the figure—cadmium yellow and yellow ochre.

Some people who are told they can't do something - rather than being consumed with doubt - it lights their fire. Others are persuaded by prevailing doubt that it can't be done and their fire is doused with doubt.

Lack of Confidence. "I'd use a palette knife on that tree." *Oh, no, another opinion.* She picked up the knife, dipped it into the paint, and began to dab at the tree. *I haven't had enough experience with a palette knife,* she thought. *This isn't at all what I wanted.* But by now she was losing confidence in her own opinion. The professor passed by and smiled at her, encouraging her to continue. She started again and finally finished the area around the figure she had sketched in. She picked up a brush and started on her image.

Comparison. The minutes passed painfully

slowly as her portrait began to take shape: lighter color on her nose; shade in the corners of the eyes, below the chin, defining the form. She glanced at the student nearest her who was also painting a portrait. *He's good. His looks three-dimensional. Mine seems flat. What a mess. How could I possibly think I was ready for this? Maybe I don't have the right kind of brushes,* she thought. *No, they're the best I could get. Maybe there's a glare on the canvas. Is the paint too thin? She looked at the photo. No, it's not me, it's the photo.*

Conflict. *Here comes the professor.* She wanted to hide her inferior efforts. She began to feel a sense of panic. *I don't want him to see this mess. He's had high hopes for me.* She reached down to pick up one of the rags she'd brought. I'm going to wipe this off and start over. Whoops! The rag flew out of her hand. She bent to pick it up. Too late. The professor stood next to her, looking at what she perceived to be an embarrassingly poor beginning.

Quietly he picked up a brush, dipped it into the paint, and made a couple of dabs at the painting, then took her unsteady hand and carefully guided her brush. Incredibly self-conscious, filled with doubt, she took a deep breath and willed her trembling hands to follow his silent example. He walked away to another student as she continued doing what he suggested.

The minutes crawled by as she dabbed, brushed, feathered, wiped away small sections and repainted. After a while she stood back to get a better view of her work, then glanced around at the other artists. They all seemed to be doing so much better. She made a couple more swipes at the canvas. Then laid down her brush. *It's no good. I should have done a bowl of fruit.* Her confidence level had reached an all-time low by the time the professor came around again. "This is a good beginning," he said. "You've got a good foundation, your proportions are correct, you have all the right materials, keep at it. I'll be here to help you; you don't have to do it all at once. Take your time. Remember what I've told you and trust me. Just as you are working on this masterpiece to fulfil its potential, so am I working on you. You are also a masterpiece in the making."

She was truly startled at the professor's words. She wondered, *Could it be that I am finally beginning to catch on to what the teacher is trying to show me? Will this mess really turn out to be an image of what I know I should be?*

Complaints. This art student struggled to hold onto her insight and personal joy as she tried to ignore her critics and joy-robbers. The biggest critic and joy-robber of our portrait in progress is Satan. He does everything he can to cause us to disbelieve that we can ever be made into the likeness of Jesus Christ, our Redeemer. He uses critics. He erodes our confidence. He saturates us with doubt. He draws our focused attention on those who are "better" than we are. Those relentless voices within us weaken our resolve. The Bible tells us that he even runs to God and puts our blemishes on display. However, we have an Advocate who stands at God's right hand and defends us by His own righteousness. Remember, "The one who is in you [Christ, the Master Artist] is greater than the one who is in the world [Satan, the Accuser]" (1 John 4:4). When we realize that our clumsy attempts at painting our self-portraits are gradually being corrected and perfected by the Master Artist, we will discover incredible freedom and inner peace. Our inadequacies and insecurities are simply aspects of a portrait in progress. **Converting Messes into Masterpieces.** Early in life, literally thousands of young men and women have spilled paint, dropped brushes, or ignored the leading of the Master Artist. And, tragically, those self-motivated and sin-caused mistakes in life, exaggerated by criticisms from others, created voices within fueling feelings of inadequacy and insecurity. Our natural response is to use the tools of this world: money, beauty, fame and the approval of others to protect ourselves. Our spiritual response is to commit ourselves to the painstaking and patient process of being a masterpiece in the making.

If we allow Him to help us with the finishing touches, He will turn our messes into masterpieces that reflect His image. When we realize that God is still at work in us, we can resist being manipulated by circumstances, media messages, opinions of others, or voices from the Accuser that so often remind us that we just don't measure up. Praise God! You're free to paint!

RESTORATION

The year was 1498. The twenty-three-year-old Florentine sculptor signed a unique contract. He agreed to complete, in marble, within one year, a statue of the Pieta (figures of Mary holding her crucified Son on her lap) that would be housed in the papal cathedral of St. Peter's in Rome. In the contract he promised that the figure of Christ would be "of the size of a proper man" and the work would be done "for the price of 450 ducats of the papal mint." He had already done a number of sculptures, none of which attracted much attention.

As he began to chip away at the massive piece of marble, the young sculptor envisioned the dead Christ draped across His mother's lap differently than other artists had. It would not be stark and grisly; rather, he interpreted the Christ as if He were merely asleep, as if to suggest that He will rise again. The mother's left hand expresses both grief at her great loss, but also acceptance that her

Son was crucified for the benefit of the world. One year later, true to his word, the sculptor presented the completed statue. It immediately became the object of much admiration. The figures were finished to a degree of refinement and subtlety that was unmatched at that time. For the first and perhaps the last time, the young man signed his name to his work, recognizing that it well could be his greatest endeavor. On the band that lay diagonally along the mother's breast, in Latin, he carved "Michelangelo Buonarroti the Florentine made it."

For nearly five hundred years, visitors to the chapel in Rome quietly, reverently, and contemplatively gazed at the magnificent *Pieta*. Then, one day in 1972, evil and insanity invaded the chapel when a man savagely attacked the *Pieta* with a hammer, damaging the mother's face. The man was arrested, and all the pieces of the sculpture were collected and saved. Carefully and painstakingly Vatican conservators restored the statue. Today, visitors can once again view the sculpture behind bullet-proof glass, sealed against the onslaught of any who would destroy this masterpiece.

Carefully and faithfully, God is putting the finishing touches on our hearts and lives. He never gives up. He promises to complete the portrait. He has built a "Satan-proof" protection around us. We can count on his protection as He continues the restoration process. Perhaps this song will illustrate the essence of God's Divine plan to make us into His image.

◆

There really ought to be a sign upon my heart:
"Don't judge me yet, There's an unfinished part!"
But I'll be perfect just according to His plan,
fashioned by the Master's lovin' hand.
He's still workin' on me to make me what I ought to be.
It took Him just a week to make the moon and stars,
The sun and the earth and Jupiter and Mars.
How loving and patient He must be!
He's still workin' on me.[1]

◆

PERSONAL EVALUATION
&
PRACTICAL APPLICATION

I found this self-image inventory in my files over thirty years ago when I was a youth pastor. The only name I found as a source was Ken Williams, and I certainly want to acknowledge his good work. This inventory will provide a practical way for you to identify areas in your own life that may need to be placed back on the easel of God's portrait in progress. It will also help you read this book with a sense of awareness of what areas in your life need the most attention.

Self-Image Inventory

Use the following system to rate yourself on each question:

a. Definitely yes or almost always	3
b. Probably yes or often	2
c. Probably not or seldom	1
d. Definitely not or almost never	0

1. I am happy with my physical appearance. _____
2. I can accomplish almost any task I attempt. _____
3. I feel as worthwhile when I'm just having a good time as when. I'm working hard on a task. _____
4. I consider my ability to think and reason adequate. _____
5. I think most people find my personality pleasant. _____
6. I can forgive myself for past sins. _____
7. When I make a mistake, I refrain from telling myself that I am dumb, stupid, can't do anything right or other negative remarks. _____
8. I can honestly say that I love myself. _____
9. I feel that God looks on me with favor rather than disfavor. _____

10. I am satisfied with the degree of success I am experiencing so far in my life. _____
11. When I look at myself in the mirror I like what I see. _____
12. I feel competent to take on most jobs or challenges. _____
13. Being a child of God, I feel of great value and worth as a person, even when I fail. _____
14. I am happy with the level of my intelligence. _____
15. Generally, I feel good about my personality. _____
16. When I sin and confess it to God, I find that I am free from self-condemning thoughts. _____
17. When I talk to myself (as everyone does), it is usually positive about myself rather than critical. _____
18. I can appreciate and love myself even though I am far from perfect. _____
19. Though I realize I am a sinner, down deep I can truly feel that God sees me as holy and blameless through Christ. _____
20. Overall I would regard myself as successful in life. _____

Scoring of Self-Image Inventory
Write your total score here: _____

Total Score Assessment
56-60   If you scored in this range, chances are you either faked the inventory or you see yourself more highly than you ought to.

46-55   You seem to have a high estimation of yourself and should have few problems with self-esteem, unless you scored par ticularly low in one or more specific areas.

36-45   Overall, you appear to be neither high nor low in self-esteem, but there may be specific areas whichneed attention.

26-35   There is considerable room for improvement in your self-image.

1-25   If you were honest in the questionnaire, you have urgent need for improvement.

Please note that you will refer back to this for another evaluation at the end of chapter two.

1. Identify three of the most dominant "inner voices" that limit your freedom.

    A._____

    B._____

    C._____

2. What specific aspects in your view of self can you begin to change?

3. What are some ways to deal with relationships with significant others who generally criticize or point out your weaknesses?

    A._____

    B._____

    C._____

4. Does Satan constantly remind you of past failures? How can a person get free from condemning messages supplied by Satan and magnified by self?

5. What can be done regarding people who have in the past or are presently injuring your view of self?

2

THE MAKEUP

Image Projecting Masks

As the artist proceeded with her portrait, she noticed how her perspectives were changing. She paused and reflected on the work she had accomplished. She saw this portrait differently than when she started. The need to project an image that she thought would bring approval from others diminished. With further examination of her efforts she realized how her thoughts were beginning to reflect those of the professor. She pressed forward to portray an accurate depiction of how she saw herself when the masks were removed. She was filled with an excitement and anticipation about seeing her real self. On the other hand she had considerable fear about removing masks. She saw that once all of her personal biases and doubts were dissolved, she was able to proceed with the process just as the professor instructed. *This is what the professor wanted me to see and experience: the potential he sees and to experience the joy of the process free from personal, image-projecting masks.*

At an early age we all begin to do what we can to make ourselves look the best we can. That is very natural and is to be expected. We are primarily concerned in this book with the personal, emotional, and spiritual efforts to cover our blemishes; most are not wrong or harmful. But if our efforts to cover and protect our image keep us from cooperating with the Master, then they can interfere with the process and slow the progress of our portrait. We call these "image projecting masks."

When I was a child I watched movies of soldiers jumping out of planes and drifting to the ground in parachutes. I thought that would be exciting! After high school my older brother Larry went into the Army Paratroopers and served in a Special Forces unit in Viet Nam. I was so proud of him and decided to follow in his footsteps. I was eighteen years old when I arrived at the US Army Paratrooper Training Camp, determined to become the best of the army elite.

Although I didn't know it at the time, the drill sergeants' vocational obsession for the first week of training was to break us down. They let us know that we could do nothing right. We paid for our mistakes by doing hundreds of push-ups. We began each day by standing at attention by our bedsides while the sergeant tossed a silver dollar onto our bunk beds. If the bed was not made tight enough for the coin to bounce high enough for him to catch (it seemed he didn't try very hard sometimes), he would rip off the covers and demand that we make it right, just as soon as we had completed a series of push-ups. By the second day, nearly everyone was tense and fearful from the mental harassment and emotional intimidation.

In just a few days, we were stripped of all of our image-projecting masks. Whatever we had routinely used to protect our inner insecurities was totally dismantled. It didn't matter how we saw ourselves. We were exposed. We were reduced to the basics. No place to hide. No impressive image.

The sergeants' ultimate goal seemed to be to confront us with incredible challenges that would make it impossible for us to succeed and force us to leave the training grounds totally humiliated. But we did not understand that the immense pressure was actually a prerequisite to rebuilding us. It was intended to instill courage, confidence, and camaraderie in all who survived. The sergeants knew that these personal traits were critical ingredients in the making of a paratrooper. They were determined to "create" the kind of soldier that all would be proud and confident to serve with – especially when risking your life in combat.

On day three, the drill sergeants lined us up to explain the use of the reserve parachute. I stood frozen at attention and listened intently as he described the basics. Sounded simple enough. A reserve parachute is simply an extra parachute you harness onto your chest. If your main chute does not deploy (shortly after a desperate prayer), you grab this nice shiny handle and pull. The secondary parachute opens and there is a good chance you will live to tell the story. I suppose that particular aspect of the training session was supposed to quiet our fears of the "what-ifs."

The entire class lined up to receive their reserve parachutes. The drill sergeants yelled for us to run (you did not walk anyplace on the training ground) by the equipment supply center. The sergeants tossed a parachute at each man as he ran by, throwing it so that it was hard to catch. It was sheer pandemonium. Troopers were doing push-ups all over the place for missing their chutes. I lined up. I ran with focused determination to catch the chute no matter how bad the pass. The chute came flying at me. I caught it! Glory! I took off running! But in all the confusion of the moment I grabbed the nice shiny handle and pulled. The chute fell to the ground. I stopped, stared at the handle, and started to look behind me. OOPS! My parachute was deploying, popping out behind me in a long flowing sheet along the ground. (Now a word from my over-active imagination.) The troopers all around doing push-ups for a variety of mess-ups looked my way with what seemed an attitude of gratitude. EVERY-ONE looked at me. I had no place to hide. My mind rapidly reviewed the terrifying scenarios of what would happen next. Talk about feeling inadequate and insecure!

Three sergeants ordered me to approach. I knew how excited they were to use me as a demonstration.

Drop and do fifty push-ups!

Had enough, soldier?

No, Sir! I bellowed back at him! (I lied.)

Do fifty more!

Today, as I look back at that thoroughly humiliating experience and exhausting paratrooper training - I see the parallel in my Christian experience. I realize that a prerequisite to developing a strong, healthy and biblical sense of self is being willing to identify and rid ourselves of image-projecting masks. Un-masking is often the result of being challenged to the limits of our abilities. They can be viewed as opportunities, not obstacles, as blessings rather than blemishes on our self-portrait.

◆

Difficult circumstances in life do not make statements about who we are. They are the opportunities for creating the kind of person God would be proud to serve with in the heat of spiritual warfare.

◆

Just like the beginning artist, if you cannot overcome the voices within and the critics all around who are willing to point out your obvious mistakes, it will slow the progress of the portrait. Being preoccupied with our weaknesses makes it difficult to cooperate with the Master Artist. In essence, we do all that we can to cover our incomplete portrait.

I recall a young couple who came to the ALIVE counseling center for marriage counseling. The husband declared at the outset that he was from the "old school" and admittedly did not show his wife much affection or respect. After nearly three months of individual and couple counseling, it became very apparent that he behaved the way he did toward his wife because of his own inner insecurities and feelings of inadequacy. He and his wife began to understand that his insensitivity, lack of affirmation and love were not intentionally mean. But to some extent it was the little boy inside that believed he had to be in control and be tough as a way of protecting himself. That motivated his behavior. The dynamics in the marriage took on a whole new perspective. He began to risk his insecurities and she began to encourage him instead of criticize him. I knew this couple very well. As they both recommitted to cooperate with the Master, their marriage relationship began to be a true reflection of a masterpiece in the making.

In the spiritual realm, being fashioned into the image of God is a lifetime process – requiring faith-driven patience. That is why it is so easy to notice the blemishes and want to hide them. Isn't it curious that, almost without exception, when we first see photographer's proofs of a formal family portrait, each of us points out what we don't like about our own expression, clothes, or posture? If there are six people in the family – there will likely be six different opinions about which of the pictures is best. Trying to select the picture that everybody is pleased with can sometimes lead to conflict. When we choose to point out what we don't like about ourselves, we miss the bigger picture.

PROTECTION – NOT DECEPTION

People who hide behind masks do not do so to deceive others but to protect the inner person wearing them. We think that if we distract those around us with masks and makeup they will not be able to see our insecurities and inadequacies. We hope that wearing masks will protect us from these nagging faults that interfere with our lives. And they do somewhat insulate us from tormenting self-conscious doubts.

Unfortunately, Christians who are fearfully and wonderfully made do this as much as or more than people who do not know the Master Artist. Because we are afraid of not measuring up to others' expectations, and as Christians what God expects, we hide behind the masks to please them and protect ourselves. We do not want other Christians to think badly of us. After awhile, our insecurities and inadequacies are buried so deep that we do not recognize the mask we have on at any particular time. In some sense, the more masks we wear, the less likely we will be motivated to continue the maturing process. Wearing masks soothes the pain and discomfort of being incomplete and literally robs us of our motivation to cooperate with the Master Artist who is in pursuit of perfection. What are some of the more familiar masks?

The Piety Mask. The dictionary defines "piety" as "dutiful-ness in religion." Jesus rebuked those Pharisees who, "on the outside, appeared righteous but would, in an effort to disguise their own hypocrisy and wickedness...tie up heavy loads and put them on [others]" (Matthew 23:28,4). Often, a "Piety" mask is worn by the Christian who is critical of another Christian whose walk is not as "Christ-like" as the pious person believes it should be. The wearer of this mask is hoping that, by pointing out the blemishes of others, he can distract everyone else from his own. Jesus condemned this attitude in the Pharisees. He called them "whitewashed tombs" – not a flattering title.

Sometimes, people who want to be accepted into the Christian community without going through the rebirth process put on this mask. They join a church and become involved in a variety of church activities without ever having a personal relationship with God. They learn acceptable words of prayer but never seriously talk to God. They teach the Bible but never hide God's Word in their hearts so that it changes their lives. They worship and praise just as the others do but never know the joy that true praise brings. The tragedy is that they are not aware that they have become content with pretending.

I recall a counseling intake interview with a young woman who seemed overly spiritual. She did not want to talk about anything except her relationship with the Lord. She would bring her "jumbo size" Bible to the session and keep the focus on spiritual and theological issues. All the while it became increasingly evident that she was genuinely longing to talk about her heartfelt pain. Her father was a pastor and she learned early that it was important to put on a spiritual mask as a way to encourage others and "be a good example." Others around her would applaud her for her good testimony and positive attitude, but she felt isolated and lonely. She wanted to tell somebody how she really felt inside but was afraid she would be misunderstood, disappoint others, and embarrass her father. She was desperately lonely but found it terrifying to be honest with God, Dad, and self, so she kept her mask of piety in place. Her mask was intended to project an acceptable image as a way of protecting herself – not to deceive others.

Not always, but often when someone is loudly and dramatically declaring his righteousness, he is simply doing what he can to hide the truth about himself from himself. And most often, such people convince others of their spiritual depth, but are never able to quiet the voices of doubt and criticism in their own hearts. This means you don't have to pretend or wear masks. Our trust in God allows us to be honest with ourselves and transparent with others. **The Physical Mask.** Some wear a pious mask to appear holy. Less insidious, but still serving the same purpose, is our attempt to disguise what we physically look like to others. We don't like the person we are so we take great pains to be somebody else.

We all have a slight (or great) tendency to judge other people by their physical appearance. If we see a rugged looking man wearing a ten-gallon hat and boots with spurs, we immediately think, "cowboy." If we encounter a person who is extremely overweight we think, "heart attack." We are influenced by hundreds of years of conditioning to judge people by their outward appearance.

John the Baptist came roaring out of the desert to the Jordan River dressed in rough clothing made of camel hair, preaching: "Prepare the way for the Lord" (Matthew 3:3). This was probably his normal garb; but it attracted attention, which was what he wanted to do. We dress in our finest to attend church on Easter Sunday. Certain Christian groups wear black, avoid modern inventions, and live in closed communities. Some clergymen wear white collars to show their calling. These people all wear clothing that, at least to some extent, announces who they are. People with poor self-esteem often lose their balance and put on a physical mask that distracts others from seeing who they are on the inside.

As a matter of fact, our whole society seems to be transfixed with altering their physical appearance. The fitness craze proves that. Exercise equipment is widely used to build up or break down faulty body parts. Many teens become anorexic or bulimic to look thin. Cosmetic surgery is commonplace. Store shelves are filled with new medications and ancient herbs that promise slim figures or perpetual youth. We are obsessed with changing our physical appearance because we are unhappy with the way we look.

On a recent popular talk show, a woman shared that she had undergone nine plastic surgeries. When asked if she finally felt satisfied/content, she said, "I'm getting there." Many people have surgery after surgery hoping the next one will change how they feel about themselves.

This preoccupation with physical fitness and physical attractiveness is especially obvious in Hollywood. Movie stars rely on body building and cosmetic surgery to alter their outward appearances, yet many of their lives reflect inner pain and no peace. No matter what you do to your bodies, it does not get beneath your skin to your heart. Listen to what the Master Artist says in Psalm 139: "O Lord, you have searched me and you know me. You know when I sit and when I rise; you perceive my thoughts from afar. You discern my going out and my lying down; you are familiar with all my ways. Before a word is on my tongue you know it completely, O Lord" (vv. 1-4). God's concern is with our hearts, thoughts and intentions, not with our outward appearance.

Recently a professional photographer took pictures of my wife and me. There was no comparison with the snapshots we take with our own camera. What a difference a professional can make. We were both very pleased with the results. We were dressed in our best and displayed contented smiles. The photographer used the proper lighting, flattering color tones, and an interesting background. He airbrushed away the wrinkles and blemishes. He captured the outer images we wanted to see.

Don't misunderstand me. I am not saying there's anything wrong with looking your best or with self-improvement. But it is wrong if you become obsessed with the outside in order to mask who you are within. Masking keeps you from changing within.

I did a little informal experiment with this idea of how impressed people are with how we look. Each year I teach in the graduate school at Moody Bible Institute in Chicago. On one occasion they sent a young student to pick me up at the airport and I just couldn't resist being ornery. I put a magnetic earring on and shoved specially made bucked teeth in my mouth. Wow! As the student helped me with my luggage I intentionally talked to him so that he had to pay attention to my protruding teeth and slurred speech. He kept looking, listening, and wondering what Moody had come to. In just a few short minutes I let him off the hook. He was so relieved he laughed for a long time and repeatedly talked about what he was thinking and how he didn't know what to say. We all develop preconceived notions about the way certain people should look and are jolted when our notions prove to be wrong.

The Personal Achievement Mask. You will recall that most of us learn early in life that our value is measured by the approval and affirmation of significant others. We set out on a relentless journey to win the approval of others. Even those who are reluctant to approve have to acknowledge our achievements.

Sometimes we can become so consumed with success and achievement that we have little interest or time for character and spiritual development. Some hide behind the personal achievement masks of celebrity, skill, or success. Of celebrity—the movie star who is recognized everywhere he or she goes, to the point of being afraid to appear in public; of skill — the baseball pitcher who commands a $15 million annual salary; of success—the computer magnate whose annual salary could support several small third-world countries. If these achievers are wearing masks, sooner or later that mask will slip and reveal significant self-doubts.

The real person is more than his profession or fame. That is true whether an entertainer, sports figure, successful businessperson, skilled surgeon, or the president of the United States. If there is no depth of character, the real self will one day be on display for all to see. You can count on that.

Jesus gave His followers an illustration that is similar to this "Personal Achievement" Mask. "To some who were confident of their own righteousness and looked down on everybody else, Jesus told this parable: 'Two men went up to the temple to pray, one a Pharisee and the other a tax collector. The Pharisee stood up and prayed about himself; "God, I thank you that I am not like all other men, robbers, evildoers, adulterers or even like this tax collector. I fast twice a week and give a tenth of all I get." But the tax collector stood at a distance. He would not even look up to heaven, but beat his breast and said, "God, have mercy on me, a sinner." I tell you that this man, rather than the other, went home justified before God. For everyone who exalts himself will be humbled, and he who humbles himself will be exalted'" (Luke 18:9-14). Personal achievements, though good in themselves, cannot fully satisfy our inner longing to become more and more like the heavenly model for our personal portrait.

The Peer Acceptance Mask. Peer acceptance -- whether as a member of a gang or church choir is a powerful motivation behind many important decisions. The teenage years are a time when young adults are searching for their true identity and are especially vulnerable to this important need. They look to their peers more often than to their families to define what is acceptable, "cool." Some experiment with drugs and alcohol or compromise their sexual integrity because they want to be accepted by their friends. They paint portraits of themselves dressed in the same faddish clothing their peers buy, wearing the latest acceptable hairstyles, and behaving in ways that make their parents wonder, "What has happened to my wonderful child?" Others become academic achievers or outstanding athletes and feast on the affirmation and recognition of their peers. One talented teenager's father continually put him down, comparing him to his sisters who were "perfect." He suffered both emotional and physical abuse. It became so bad that the young man sought his acceptance in the drug culture of his peers. But no matter how abusive or disruptive his behavior became, his mother, aunt, grandmother, and sisters loved him, nurtured him, and counseled him. They didn't believe in "tough love." When he ended up one night in the emergency ward because of a bad drug, he began to hear the love-motivated messages. The negative ones his father had instilled in his heart began to diminish. Today he is married to his long-time girlfriend and is making a success of his life. More importantly, he recognizes that the Master Artist is creating a masterpiece.Wearing various masks to protect us from the truth about our self-conscious doubts results in short-term gain and long-term pain. It deals with the symptoms but not the sources. Pretending keeps us from the work of painting.

---◆---

**Seeing ourselves as a masterpiece in the making gives
us freedom to remove our masks.**

---◆---

GRADING ON THE CURVE

The truth is that most adults are not so far removed from our early childhood reflections on the grade-card we receive from others. In some ways there is a "little boy or little girl" inside that is always monitoring how we appear to others. We want so much that others will graciously grade us on the curve. Our adult image-projecting masks are more sophisticated and socially appropriate. We often send strong messages to others of our worth through the clothes we wear, the type of car we drive, our home, education, employment, and a myriad of other visible clues about our worth. These normal experiences and desires in life are a problem only if they serve the primary purpose of hiding the "real you" from yourself and others.

A good friend and ministry partner, Ken Davis, gives his testimony of how God enabled him to overcome serious insecurities and feelings of inferiority. Throughout his growing-up years and well into his adult life he had constant battles with negative messages about his worth.

During a desperate time in his life he did not even want to live any longer. He cried out to God. Little by little God began to allow Ken to see himself as God saw him. He experienced an incredible liberation. Today, his worldwide ministry is characterized by the ability to see his faults and failures from God's perspective. His ability to laugh at some of his limitations has been the most refreshing and encouraging aspect of his ministry. Ken declares with boldness his love for God. He declares with spiritual discernment his confidence that God is re-creating him into His image. Ken acknowledges that knowing the unconditional love of Christ means it is no longer necessary to pretend or project impressive images. It is his transparency, vulnerability and genuinely authentic style that communicates his freedom in Christ. It is his willingness to publicly "un-mask" his own fears and insecurities that becomes a powerful motivation for others to remove their masks and meet the Master. He says that once he began to catch on to this great truth he realized he had nothing to hide, nothing to gain and nothing to lose. I am who I am in Christ! His transparent heart of love for God and zest for life is contagious and has impacted lives all around the world. He is indeed a reflection of the Lord Jesus Christ – He is a master-piece in the making.

PERSONAL EVALUATION
&
PRACTICAL APPLICATION

This test measures ten different factors of self-esteem. Two questions relate to each of the ten factors. Write your total score on each factor.
Please refer to the questions in the Self-Image Inventory at the end of chapter one.

Factor	Question For Factor	Total Score
1. Appearance	1,11	_____
2. Competence	2,12	_____
3. Unconditional worth	2,13	_____
4. Intelligence	4,14	_____
5. Personality	5,15	_____
6. Self-forgiveness	6,16	_____
7. Acceptance of weakness	7,17	_____
8. Self-love	8,18	_____
9. Freedom from guilt	9,19	_____
10. Success	10,20	_____

If your score was two or below for any one factor, you will want to work on developing your self-image in that area. Remember: This questionnaire can be helpful, but the results of a single, simplified test are not enough for a true evaluation. If you scored very low do not conclude you are a failure. Don't over-emphasize the result of the inventory. No test of this nature is capable of adequately describing the self-image of every person who takes it. But if you did score in the lower range you may want to talk it over with a Christian counselor.

Take a few minutes to review the self-test and discussion questions:

1. What is the most prominent mask you wear? Why do you wear this mask?

2. What are the top three reasons for the various masks you wear?

   A._____
   B._____
   C._____

3. Can you remember a time when you "unmasked" and were hurt or offended? In contrast, were you genuinely encouraged?

4. Think about three people who had a powerful and positive influence in how you view yourself.

   A._____
   B._____
   C._____

5. Like Ken Davis, we all need to move toward trust and transparency. With whom could you risk being yourself? Are you ready to be confident and remove you masks?

3

THE MODEL

Image-Protecting Myths

Slowly, she repositioned the brush in her hands, focused on the next phase of her portrait. With her breath held, she began again with a contagious confidence captured from her professor. *If he thinks that I can do this - that I have talent to fulfill this task, then I can continue. After all, he knows what he is talking about. All I have to do is remember his words of instruction and encouragement.* Once again she is proving her potential. She continued with boldness.

But wait. What happened? Her strokes became shaky, unnatural. As her hands began to tremble with nerves, she could hear the echoes of each heartbeat in her head. *Look how far behind I am. Why is mine taking so long? Mine will never be as aesthetically pleasing as the others.* The questions and doubt continued. Soon the questions turned from self-comparison to doubt - doubt of her talent and of the professor. *He must have known how behind I was when he came around. How could he encourage me about my potential?* Her mind no longer heard his encouragement and profitable instruction; all she could focus on was her constant comparison to the others in the class. She struggled to continue, *What is true - what I see or what I was told by the professor?*

This tension in our lives and hearts about how we see ourselves, at least in part, is a direct result of the passionate conflict between the Master Artist and the master of deceit – Satan himself. He provides a steady diet, especially through TV, pop culture, radio and magazines of easily believed myths about the important ingredients that make up a beautiful portrait of self.

Many untruths or myths contribute to painful feelings of not measuring up. And it is easy to become manipulated by various myths that motivate us to protect certain "esteem building" images. These myths, proclaimed over and over in our own thoughts and words, keep alive the doubts we have about our real self. Some of them are:

- If I'm not blessed with money, possessions, intelligence... I am nobody.
- If I'm not beautiful, handsome, thin, tall, athletic, strong, ... I will not be accepted.
- If I make a fool of myself in public... no one will like me.
- If I come from a dysfunctional family... I'm scarred for life.
- If I've ever been neglected, rejected, abused... I can never fully recover.

Perhaps some additional ones that we would say as Christians are:

- If I don't preach Jesus to everyone I meet... Jesus won't claim me as one of His.
- If I commit that same sin one more time... God is going to give up on me.
- If I don't take on that job I'm asked to do, even though I'm already overextended... people will think I'm a shirker.

- If people know I'm divorced... I'll be excluded from fellowship.

Add your own myth messages. What do you play over and over in your own mind that could be contributing to a discouraging perspective of yourself? Many of these myths are planted within you by the master of deceit himself. He doesn't want you to believe that you are "fearfully and wonderfully made" by the Master Artist. Here are some of his favorites.

I Wouldn't Be this Way if I Were Rich, Famous, Intelligent, Beautiful. The illusion that if I were rich or famous I would not have fears and negative attitudes about myself becomes even more complex for the Christian.

You may think people who are endowed with abundant blessings never struggle with feelings of insecurity or inadequacy. Or, conversely, you may believe that people who have an obviously low self-esteem are that way because they lack these gifts. Both are myths.

Several years ago a handsome, very intelligent man came to me for counseling. This man was a lawyer who had graduated with honors. After several sessions he began to transition into his real need. He haltingly expressed that he felt insecure and inferior. He was miserable and depressed because he was afraid he would not always be able to measure up to the expectations of others. He was especially anxious that his fears would someday be revealed.

He had tried to confide in one of his professional colleagues, and his friend laughed and said, "You're kidding; that's the last thing I would've thought." Then his well-intentioned friend began to list all of his credentials in an attempt to talk him out of his feelings. It did not help. In fact it made him reluctant to share his pain with anyone else. Why bother? They just would not understand. He told me, "If I don't resolve this I may spend years of my life trying to convince others of my worth without ever being able to convince myself." How tragic -- but how true.

After further counseling we began to recognize that he had a deep myth-motivated need to prove his worth. Soon he began to acknowledge that true worth comes from the eternal perspective. We are God's handiwork and a divine portrait in progress. "He who began a good work in you will carry it on to completion until the day of Christ" (Philippians 1:6).

This man began to earnestly cooperate and participate with his Creator God, the Master Artist. His negative self-evaluation began to filter through an internal and eternal, scriptural perspective. It changed his life forever.

Of course, if money or beauty or fame is your goal in life as a means to supplement your ego needs, then this is a problem. However, if God has blessed you with these gifts, He wants you to be thankful for them and allow Him to use them as a testimony of the brush marks of the Master Artist.

This myth tells us that we, as godly people, should not be concerned with material wealth, good looks, or success. For some reason we have adopted the thinking that Christians who pursue or possess these qualities did so at the cost of spiritual commitment. Special blessings from God will provide wonderful opportunities to share your faith with others and glorify God.

It's Sinful to Have a Positive Self-Image. This myth has distorted the personal image of many Christians. We are, as the original first verse of the old hymn, "At the Cross," proclaimed, just worms. Even the change in more modern hymnals does not raise us much in our own eyes. If our self-image is based on selfish pride, then it is sin. The problem with this idea is that pride and self-esteem are not necessarily the same. Sinful pride means that I think I am better than other people. Arrogance is the assumption that others agree with my inflated self-estimation. The Bible tells us not to think too highly of ourselves, to be humble (but not abased). Positive self-esteem has to do with knowing who we are as children of God.

I recall receiving a very critical letter from someone I had never met. I was an adjunct faculty member for a summer module at a seminary. The letter was first critical of the seminary for having someone teach who had a doctorate in psychology. Secondly, they noticed in my course outline that I planned to do a section on self-esteem. In this particular section of the class I would present counseling stories of many casualties in spiritual warfare that could be directly traced to distorted and destructive attitudes about self. It was sadly evident in the context of the letter they were paranoid about Christians having pride and egotistical inflated self-esteem. Their fear had resulted in a myth that kept them from knowing little of the exhilarating and liberating perspective of self – from the Master Artist's view.

Our job is to build up what God called "good" and emphasize the qualities of self that are reflective of the image of God. These qualities are expressed in Galatians 5, the "fruit of the Spirit": "Love, joy, peace, patience, kindness, goodness, faithfulness, gentleness and self-control" (vv. 22-23). This is quite a contrast to what the world says should make up a self-portrait. In no way are these qualities ego-inflating or self-serving. Quite the opposite. Paul continues in verse 26: "Let us not become conceited, provoking and envying each other." These wonderful, colorful "fruits" need to be painted onto the canvas of our self-portrait.

I Don't Have any Skills or Talents; I'm Nobody. This is the way Moses thought. How did he see himself? Well, look at his early record. Did Moses see himself as a boy growing up in Pharaoh's palace, arrayed in royal garments? Or was his image of a shepherd, tending sheep in a place the Bible calls "the far side of the desert"? Or did he discover his real self when he was face down on the ground before a bush that was burning but not consumed by the fire? How did Moses see himself? How did his Creator, God, see him?

THREE LIVES OF MOSES

Moses truly led three lives. And as we study those lives we see how God was preparing him for one of the greatest tasks in Israel's long history. When it came time for Moses to do this task, he began to backpedal. The evidence of Moses' keen awareness of his limitations and inability to see himself through the eyes of God unfold in this dramatic story. Listen to the conversation.

God: (declarative) "I've seen how miserable my people are in Egypt and I want you to get them out."

Moses: (surprised) "Who me? Why me? I'm nobody. The Egyptians won't listen to me. Besides, I'm afraid. Remember, I killed one of them and they might still be looking for me."

God: (patiently) "The ones who wanted to kill you are all dead. Besides, I'll be with you."

Moses: (quizzical) "The Israelites won't listen to me. They hate me because I grew up in Pharaoh's palace. Why should they trust me."

God: (majestic) "Tell them the God of your fathers—of Abraham, Isaac, and Jacob—sent you to them. I AM is sending you to them."

Moses: (doubtful) "What if they don't believe me?"

God: (convincingly) "I'll help you perform miracles that will convince them."

Moses: (pleading) "But, Lord, I never did speak Hebrew very well, even when I lived there. And I haven't even conversed in Egyptian for forty years."

God: (angry now) "Who made your mouth? I will help you speak and will tell you what to say."

Moses: (whining) "Oh, please, God. Send somebody else."

God: (the final word) "Your brother Aaron, the priest, knows how to speak to both Israelites and Egyptians. He can talk for you. Now get ready to go and meet Aaron; he's already on his way here to see you."

Talk about not being able to see the finished portrait. Moses was not aware of the work of the Master Artist in every circumstance of his life. But God knew what kind of person Moses truly was. He created him and He had a great commission for him; the greatest commission anyone could ever have: to assure that God's plan for salvation of mankind would continue. God had called the Hebrew people His people, those who would worship only Him and from whom the Savior of the world would come. The Hebrew people had to get back to the land that God had promised would be theirs. And Moses was the one who was commissioned to take them back. That commission was very critical, and it was the greatest challenge Moses would ever receive; one with far-reaching, eternal conse-quences. God knew that Moses was capable of fulfilling it as long as he willingly placed himself on the eternal easel of the Master Artist.

Each one of us is also commissioned by God to do some-thing with our lives. If we worry about our inadequacies and insecurities we soon forget how we are fearfully and wonderfully made. We need to rip off the masks of distorted self-images and strip off the cloaks of deceit; we need to recognize the great lies we are fed every day that prevent us from realizing the full potential of our uniqueness.

Once you determine to put your real self on the Master Artist's easel, all of these qualities take on a new perspective. They are important in themselves, but are not the final word about who we are in Christ. And like Moses we must acknowledge the faithful work of God on our life portrait through impossible assignments and challenging life circumstances.

◆

Spiritual vitality, success in life, physical attractiveness, and acceptance by others are clearly desirable qualities of life.

◆

BEFORE AND AFTER

Remember the professional photographer who took pictures of Marlene and me? Instead of filming us at our best, what if he had come to our home in the early morning to take our picture? Before we brushed our teeth, combed our hair, took a shower, or had any coffee? Before Marlene had put on makeup or I had shaved?

Imagine looking at a mantel with two eight-by-ten portraits of yourself. On the left is a self-portrait, just the way you are, as incomplete as that may currently be. It is not a pretty picture because it shows all the selfishness, insecurity, and self-consciousness inside you. This "before" portrait, without professional touchup, is simply an indication that the Master Artist still has to make some finishing touchups.

The portrait to the right of our imaginary mantel is one that is being completed in you with the help of the Master Artist. If we hand Him the brush and trust Him, He will change the "before" into something that is truly beautiful.

Glenda Palmer, a friend and author, wrote a short poem

about how God uses impossible and challenging circumstances that help us rid ourselves of masks and myths.

◆

**God shattered my plate-glass life,
then He gathered up the broken pieces
and made them into wind chimes.**

◆

The New Living Translation of Ephesians 2:10 says: "For we are God's masterpiece. He has created us anew in Christ Jesus, so that we can do the good things he planned for us long ago."

The life of Helen Keller shows what can happen when reality is revealed to a physically blind person. Ann Sullivan arrived in Alabama to accept a position of tutoring a seven-year-old girl who was born deaf and blind. It shocked Ann to find a wild vixen who uttered unintelligible animal sounds. When enraged, the girl snatched dishes and threw them and herself around as though she were possessed by a demon. Many thought there was no hope. Here is Helen Keller's later description of what began to change her:

"It happened at the well-house, where I was holding the mug under the spout. Annie pumped water into it, and when the water gushed out into my hand she kept spelling w-a-t-e-r into my other hand with her fingers. Suddenly I understood. Caught up in my first joy, I reached out eagerly to Annie's ever-ready hand, begging for new words to identify whatever objects I touched. Spark after spark of meaning flew from hand to hand."2

Ann Sullivan recognized that Helen had unlimited possibilities for thinking and feeling. By the age of ten, Helen was writing to famous persons all over Europe in French. She quickly mastered five languages.

Many of us, like Helen Keller, are restless, frustrated, and agitated because we are not able to see ourselves as God does. We experience the same feelings of desperation. In a sense we can become deaf to the Words of the Master Artist and blind to the image He wants so much to create in our life portrait. When we begin to

34

see brief images of who we are becoming, then we can begin to envision the completion of our portrait, directed by the Master's hand. It is God's plan to remove all scars and blemishes from our portrait and to complete His image in us. First Corinthians 13:12 says, "Now we see but a poor reflection; then we shall see face to face. Now I know in part; then I shall know fully, even as I am fully known" by God.

Helen Keller's story lets us fully appreciate that some of the most beautiful features of our character are only truly known when we trust enough to rid ourselves of image-projecting masks and self-protecting myths.

PERSONAL EVALUATION
&
PRACTICAL APPLICATION

Review this brief self-test to see if any of these masks and myths manipulates you.

- I am self-critical and find it difficult to accept either compliments or constructive criticism.
- I pay too much attention to my appearance; I'm a perfectionist.
- I am excessively shy; I can't look people in the eye.
- I am afraid of close relationships.
- I cannot accept any weakness in myself, or in anyone else, for that matter.
- I avoid challenging situations.
- I envy the accomplishment and gifts of others.
- I feel a need to control people and circumstances.
- I find it difficult to love and be loved.
- I am critical of others' weaknesses and have a negative attitude toward them.
- I sometimes feel deep despair and have thoughts of suicide.
- I find it nearly impossible to forgive others and myself for failures.

How did you do? Any of these that you checked may stand in the way of seeing yourself from God's perspective. Did you notice that most of them evolve from image-protecting myths about what makes me acceptable?

1. List and discuss several specific myths that are evident in your local church.

   A._____
   B._____
   C._____

2. Are you able to identify myths in yourself or your significant others?

3. Like Moses, self-doubts are common and ordinary. Consider three specific areas in your life where self-doubt dominates.

   A._____
   B._____
   C._____

4. In your circle of family and friends, identify several personal/spiritual traits that truly reflect Christ-centeredness.

   A._____
   B._____
   C._____

5. Write down three prominent traits in your own life. Do these best reflect the world or the Master Artist?

   A._____
   B._____
   C._____

4

THE SITTING

Know the Model

A professional portrait artist lives pretty much on the commissions he receives to paint portraits of others. Before he ever takes up the pencil to begin the sketch, a good portrait artist will try to get to know his model. The more intimately he knows the model the greater he can capture precisely the true picture of his character. Everett Raymond Kinstler, who has done more than five hundred commissioned portraits, including those of US presidents, says that "your first job as an artist is to get your subject comfortable enough to allow pieces of their character and personality to shine through."3 The spiritual parallel is evident as we commit ourselves to see beyond the physical features to the heart. God, the Master Artist, knows us perfectly; and the more intimately we know the model for our life portrait, the more confident we become. God is both Master Artist and Perfect Model. We are His image-bearers.

Between commissions, many artists practice on their own image. Most of the "masters" painted several portraits of themselves at various ages. How would you go about painting yourself? How well do you know you? How do you see yourself? How well do you know the Master Model? Sometimes you may feel as if your portrait would be something that Dali might have done, with parts of yourself sliding off the canvas into oblivion; or a Picasso, with one eye in the middle of your forehead and your chin falling off your shoulder. Obviously not very attractive or appealing.

Now quite obviously, God the Master Artist does not need to practice. But it's important for us to study carefully how we view ourselves. We cannot fully appreciate the subtle changes the Master Artist is making unless we have an idea of how we now see ourselves.

When you look in a mirror do you see yourself the way you believe others see you, or do you see yourself the way the Master Artist and Creator sees you? Do you know how God sees you? David did: "For you created my inmost being; you knit me together in my mother's womb. I praise you because I am fearfully and wonderfully made; your works are wonderful, I know that full well. My frame was not hidden from you when I was made in the secret place. When I was woven together in the depths of the earth, your eyes saw my unformed body. All the days ordained for me were written in your book before one of them came to be" (Psalm 139:13-16).

David had many negative life-impact experiences that could have become the dominant blemishes through which he viewed himself. But his testimony demonstrates that he kept his eyes on the Master Artist instead of his major messes.

What a glorious Bible statement of our worth from God's perspective! You are God's unique creation. He knows all about you and He still loves you and has a plan for your life. He takes personal responsibility for putting the final touches on your portrait; He tells you that you too are "fearfully and wonderfully made." When you neglect to acknowledge this you diminish God's creation.

GETTING COMFORTABLE FOR THE SITTING
When an artist is commissioned to paint a portrait, he wants to bring out the very best of the model, to show the model's true, attractive character and personality. Myriad influences have helped shape the inner character of the model. His life is a reflection of significant role models and his countenance depicts his self-image. The more the artist and model know of these life-shaping dynamics, the more precise he will incorporate them into the final portrait. Additionally, in order for the artist to capture the essence of the model, it is important that the model be relaxed and comfortable.

How many times has someone taken a snapshot of you, and when you saw the finished product your self-esteem took a real nose-dive? Most of us pray we're never stopped by the highway patrol for an infraction because we'd have to pull out our driver's license and expose the terrible photo on it! And you barely recognize

40

the person who stares back at you from your passport. The same fears and feelings dominate when we, like Moses, are confronted with our incomplete and imperfect self. In your growing-up years it's quite common to be focused on self. But most of us even in our adult years can readily identify lingering evidence of this way of thinking. Being self-conscious makes it impossible for us to relax for the portrait sitting. We become restless and anxious when we focus on our weaknesses, liabilities, and perceived failures.

PERFORMANCE UNDER PRESSURE

A recent drama in my life exposes these filters of the flesh. My wife Marlene, our daughter Kara and I were returning from a trip together. We got home in the early hours of the morning. The next morning I started on my chores at home that had accumulated in our absence. I was busy with mowing the lawn and cleaning the garage. Marlene walked outside with a cup of coffee for me and noticed our truck was missing. My immediate thought was that my son Mark had borrowed it. After a few calls we assumed it had been stolen.

About three weeks later, Kara and I were on our way to school and work and stopped at our local 7-Eleven Food Store for a cup of coffee. We were shocked to see our truck parked in front of the store. After making sure it was our truck I ran into the store and confronted the driver. My adrenaline was pumping like crazy. Now I know what you're thinking. When I told this story to my friends and family they all responded with a list of: "You should haves": You should have parked behind the truck; you should have followed him and called the police; you should have...! And most of the suggestions and observations made sense to me, especially looking back. The one that appealed to me most was when someone said, "Why didn't you deck him?" – in a Christian sort of way, of course! Believe me it came very close to that at the height of the confrontation in the store.

The stand-off with the driver was very tense. I suddenly became acutely aware that I had a paratrooper attitude in a fifty-five-year-old body. Dangerous combination! Kara had called 911 and I was standing by my truck, daring him to try to leave. He settled down and said that there must be a mistake; he would call his father to come down to get things straightened out. He went to the pay phone. I walked toward our car to comfort Kara; seeing a strange man driving our stolen truck was very upsetting.

The man bolted for the truck. I rushed after him. He locked the doors. I tried to smash the window with the palm of my hand. And even though it always seems to work on TV police shows – all I succeeded in doing was bruising my hand. He began to back out. I ran down the row of parked cars and jumped out in front of him. I slammed my hands down on the hood of the truck and looked at him as if to say, "I dare you!" He did! He floored the gas pedal and tried to run me down. I pushed myself away, ran to my car and began the chase. He got away. Other than that, Kara and I were having a rather routine beginning to our day!

For two nights after the encounter I couldn't sleep well. I kept replaying the story over and over again. Each time in my mind I would do something different that would result in getting my truck back. After a couple of weeks I began to realize that the reason for my being upset obviously had a lot to do with losing the truck; but something else was going on. I was upset because I felt I hadn't handled the crisis the right way. I became very self-critical. I should have responded differently. Finally, I recognized that the way I'm put together does not allow for a lot of slack – even in an adrenaline-pumping crisis. It's especially difficult if others perceive it as a failure or fault. And it seems to me that so much of this was wrapped up with how I viewed myself -- connected to child-like, self-conscious insecurity.

The police eventually recovered my truck and the thief went to jail. As for my own experience, I'm truly grateful for the reminder of how easy it is to be critical of self and distracted from a higher view of what are the truly important ingredients of a portrait in progress.

Some believe even before you're born, your self-image begins to form. The kinds of environment in which you live, work, and play affects your self-perspective. If your primary model diminishes you as a person you will have a hard time experiencing a good esteem. Consequently you may develop feelings of inferiority, fear, and intense inadequacies. This negative perspective of yourself will eventually impact your attitudes toward God, your family, and everyone else around you.

In response to a law professor's question, Jesus quoted the two greatest commandments: "'Love the Lord your God with all your heart and with all your soul and with all your mind and with all your strength.' The second is this: 'Love your neighbor as yourself'" (Mark 12:30-31). These were not in The Ten, neither did Jesus come up with these two greatest commandments just at that time; the first is from Deuteronomy 6:4; the second from Leviticus 19:18. They were God's answer all along. But notice the last part of the second commandment: love yourself. This is the key to all love: a good self-image begins with how much you love and respect God's creation— YOU. Loving the Master with all your heart is the first step toward truly loving yourself.

POWER OF PERCEPTION

Without question it is our perception in life that determines our response to life circumstances. Not so surprisingly, one of the primary warfare strategies in the Evil One's arsenal is to select only the bad things that happen and magnify them until the good things are pushed out of the picture. Our very nature makes us extremely vulnerable to this strategy because we tend to be easily intimidated by negative messages, which ultimately influence our perspective. Moses and the Hebrews fleeing Egypt provide a good example of the power of perspective. At the Red Sea the Hebrews saw only a swiftly moving body of water they could not cross, while Moses saw the other side to where God was sending them. The story of Esther shows her courage as she faced the king, not knowing if he would receive her in his court. However, Esther knew that it was in God's plan and for God's people that she address the king. In the story of David and Goliath, the army of Israel saw only a giant, but David saw a small man in comparison to His powerful God. The spies saw only giants in the land of promise, but Joshua saw God's promise. Elisha's servant saw only an enemy army with horses and chariots surrounding the city, intent on capturing Elisha; Elisha saw an army of angels on horses and in chariots of fire on the hills, protecting them. Jesus' disciples saw only an earthly kingdom; Jesus saw eternity.

How do you see yourself? What is your perspective of yourself? How you see yourself begins first with your parents' perspective; then it continues with your peers' perspective; down the road you could be affected by your church's perspective; but the only perspective that makes an eternal difference is God's perspective.

YOUR PARENTS' PERSPECTIVE

As never before I'm hearing stories from college students who've come from homes where verbal mistreatment dominated their growing-up years. Parents who did not honestly know how to parent used excessive control and verbal intimidation to insist on obedience and conformity.

In my college classroom I provide a dramatic illustration to make a permanent mark on the way the students think about parenting. In advance I plan with a student to get upset about a test score or a grade he received on a paper. We intentionally escalate the argument until it results in me yelling at him to leave the classroom. He throws the term paper in my face, upsets his chair and races out of the room! My last words as he bolts out the door – "You are not only out of this class, I'll see to it that you are out of this college!" I then put my head down in supposed embarrassment as the students hold their breath in shock. Then in just a few short seconds, I turn the overhead projector on and it reads: "Today we will discuss the impact on children of anger out of control." Then my partner in this demonstration comes back into the classroom and takes a bow. The class breaks out in obvious relief and applause. But every year this demonstration generates lengthy discussion about how modeling anger and negative messages from significant adults impacts the lives of the students.

No doubt some of you can remember clearly the impacting

messages sent to you from your parents, a teacher or coach. I was involved in athletics for years and had the privilege of having many different coaches. One stands out as a contagious encourager. My work ethic, determination, and growth in ability were evident under his leadership. Another coach was critical, never pleased, and became an expert at diagnosing what everybody on the team didn't do right. Under his leadership I was intimidated, unmotivated, and often felt like a failure.

◆

**The powerful voices of significant others
greatly influence how we see ourselves,
and chronic negative messages tend to integrate into our
adult way of seeing ourselves.**

◆

The following story is a dramatic illustration of the impact of a constant flow of negative, hurtful messages to children from troubled parents.

Psychiatrist Dr. W. Hugh Missildine, in his book Your Inner Child of the Past, describes the sessions he had with a young woman he called Annette. For months he sat and listened to this young woman hurl her inner feelings at him. "You hate me, don't you? You wish I would die. I don't mean anything to you. Don't pretend I do. You don't even know me! You're sitting there thinking how ugly I am! You're just sitting there wishing this session was over. Don't you have anything better to do? The great doctor who is such a martyr! Well, you're not a martyr to me! You're a fake, a big fake, that's all." Meanwhile, Dr. Missildine just sat there.

Annette had come to him because she was having trouble in her marriage; she was having anxiety attacks on the street and in stores; she felt ugly and stupid, when actually she was just the opposite.

Annette grew up listening to her mother say : "You're awkward and ugly. You'll never be pretty, not worth looking at. What a stupid child! What a pity I couldn't have had a decent-looking child! You fat little pig! Get out of my sight!" One time when she had taken Annette to the seashore, she said, "Look, the ocean is right there. Why don't you walk out into the ocean and just keep walking. Then I'll be rid of you!"

Of course, after many years of this verbal abuse, Annette believed that she was ugly, stupid, fat (although she only weighed a little over a hundred pounds), bad, and worthless. Annette capably managed her house and three children despite negative messages that continued. Her husband found her irritating and frequently reminded her of her shortcomings, and Annette tolerated his abuse in silent submission. She lived in a bleak and utterly lonely world.[4]

Annette's experience may seem like an extreme example. But it's not so unusual. It happens every day to children all over America. Many people have received negative messages as children and have carried them into adulthood.

SMOTHERING MOTHERING

Just recently during our college orientation days I met a parent who came to my attention because she was very upset about – well, to be honest – about everything. The staff had asked her to talk with me to see if I could help her settle down. In front of her very self-conscious and embarrassed daughter, she began to articulate her displeasure with the housing situation, academic requirements, food service, and the orientation process in general. They were from another state and finally decided to go home. In private conversation with the student it became evident that Mom was critical and negative about all of life – but especially of her daughter. Her daughter wanted to get away from home to begin the long and challenging process of discovering who she was from God's perspective. Her controlling, dominant, and critical mother had obviously contributed to her self-conscious and self-critical manner. The student subsequently called our staff with plans to attend the following semester – this time without her mother.

It's not possible to alter your past experiences. They're gone. They can't be changed. However, you have an enormous amount of freedom to alter your evaluation of your past experiences. You can evaluate and perceive the past in a biblical fashion, with an eternal perspective. You cannot alter your experiences with your parents. No matter how much you say, "I just wish my father had..." or, "If only my mother would have..." it will never change anything.

◆

Negative messages from significant others are powerful but do not have to be permanent. How you respond to negative messages is critical. You have great freedom and an awesome responsibility in managing your response in light of the Master Model.

◆

My older daughter Kendra teaches fifth grade in a Christian school. As the new school year was beginning, other teachers and staff warned her about a boy who would give her some trouble as he had his previous teachers. Kendra made it a primary prayer focus and an exciting professional challenge. Little by little she won his heart and his cooperation. He still had difficulties in paying attention. But his grades improved, his classroom demeanor was good, and his parents reported a significant change in behavior at home. Kendra is quick to remind us that it was truly a work of the Lord. She was "modeling" the love of the Master. This story is just another illustration of the power of communicating positive, encouraging, and loving messages. It is especially important for those who are already convinced they do not deserve such loving attention.

Be encouraged. You will never be free from negative voices and abusive messages from your past, but you absolutely can be free to have a perspective based on the Master's model. Praise the Lord!

It seems so appropriate to remind all of us that the voices from the past can never drown out the still small voice of the Master Artist. Listen to Him with laser sharp attention and all other voices diminish in importance.

**Before we move on let's take a brief moment to
acknowledge and salute the
multiplied millions of families that provided a warm,
loving, and encouraging role-model.
And tip our hats to the significant others who
have had a positive and powerful influence
in our lives: coaches, teammates, parents,
grandparents, and friends.**

At Christian Heritage College I teach a class on courtship and marriage. The students are required to attend Family Law court and sit in on divorce proceedings. When I review the reports they submit, I am always impressed with their renewed commitment to the permanence of marriage and renewed praise for their parents who have stayed together and who love each other. And if you're so blessed, take a moment to reflect on how blessed you are. And if you come from a broken home, determine in your heart that you will be committed to work with God in developing a healthy, Spirit-filled environment for your family. What a great privilege. Blessed indeed!

YOUR PEERS' PERSPECTIVE

Teens routinely turn to their peers for affirmation and valida-tion. Those who are not affirmed at home or by other significant adults become addicted to peer acceptance. But this phenomenon is not unique to teens. Adults, too, are very sensitive to what their peers think of them.

Counselor Lloyd H. Ahlem tells about a very lovely young woman who came to him for help. Her problem was that she was receiving so much attention from attractive men and she did not know how to respond to them. At first, Dr. Ahlem could not see what the problem was. Then she told her story. She had been born with an ugly birthmark that covered most of one side of her face. Others constantly called attention to this unsightly disfigurement. Her child-hood acquaintances, like most children, were cruel in their comments to her; adults questioned her about it. To compensate she became an ideal student, achieving honor status in nearly every school she attended. But the stares and questions continued until she longed to avoid people altogether.

After high school a large company hired her as secretary. Hoping to hide behind her work, her diligence soon brought her rewards. She received a promotion, which required more responsibility. Her new status meant interacting with a greater number of people, which brought on fear and self-consciousness. Finally, unable to handle the painful emotions, she quit work and went to college, hoping to hide among the masses of students. Before long she was recognized for her outstanding scholarship and was invited to join honor societies, again thrusting her into the public eye. More fears. She quit school and returned to work. She bounced back and forth from school to work until she finally decided to become a schoolteacher of little children. Sure enough, her outstanding work caused her classroom to become a demonstration class. She panicked. Hordes of teachers, supervisors, principals, consultants, and state officials would put her back in the public eye. At the end of the school year, she quit.

By now she had enough money to afford getting the birthmark removed. As Dr. Ahlem listened to her, he saw only a slight scar on her cheek, and she was beautiful. Now her problem was that her surgery had not resulted in her living a "normal" life; now she was being sought out because she was so attractive. She had never been asked for a date, and never had to fend off the advances of solicitous males.

All Dr. Ahlem needed to do was give her practical advice about how to play the romantic game. He says: "But the key to the real problem was to recognize that long established self-perceptions require time and opportunity for new experiences to effect change. The lovely young lady had developed the emotional habit of seeing herself as ugly. She had believed something that became untrue. But negative beliefs don't shake easily."[5]

Her voices within and peer messages made it difficult for the emotional scars and bruises in her heart to heal, even though the facial blemish was finally removed.

YOUR CHURCH FAMILY'S PERSPECTIVE

Often wounded Christians who come for professional counseling bear the scars of being the focus of gossip. They feel isolated and alienated. The "damaged goods" syndrome dominates their perception of self. But then someone kindly reminds them of who they are in Christ and of His limitless love and forgiveness.

God says that you're "fearfully and wonderfully made"; you're the best of His creation, created in His image. Sadly, so many times, even in churches where we expect to be loved and encouraged we get a steady diet of negative messages. It is certainly true that seeing ourselves apart from the wonderful grace of God is clearly a negative image to behold. But it's critical for you as a Christian to recognize that you're of real worth. The Bible tells us that we are "peculiar" (1 Peter 2:9). Modern translations use the word "chosen," which is more in line with what W. E. Vine says it means: "a purchased possession; God's own possession."6

If we view ourselves as worthless and develop a martyr complex (which we creatively package as "humility"), we will experience paralysis of the will. Too many of us utilize this distorted perspective to rationalize failure: "After all, I'm still a sinner, just one saved by grace."

Jesus never looked at His followers as if they were worms, wretched, useless, or sinful. He surrounded Himself with harlots, murderers, rebels, a tax collector, and people who lived humble lives. He kept company with fishermen, shepherds, and housewives. He also had followers who were Pharisees, a physician, and other "important" people in the community. He treated them all equally because He knew these people were willing to cooperate with the Master Artist in the process of painting a life story. "Brothers, think of what you were when you were called. Not many of you were wise by human standards; not many were influential; not many were of noble birth. But God chose the foolish things of the world to shame the wise; God chose the weak things of the world to shame the strong. He chose the lowly things of this world and the despised things and the things that are not, to nullify the things that are" (1 Corinthians 1:26-28).

God considers us "a chosen people, a royal priesthood, a holy nation, a people belonging to God, that you may declare the praises of him who called you out of darkness into his wonderful light" (1 Peter 2:9). How disappointed He must be when we do not see ourselves as royalty but, rather, we allow ourselves to be manipulated and dominated by feelings of insecurity and fears of inadequacy.

Over the years in my college ministry I have counseled with dozens of Christian young people who were literally alienated from church because they were "not in step" with the expected standards of dress or hair style, etc. One young man from the Midwest was rejected by his father and alienated from the church youth group because he wore an earring.

MODELING FORGIVENESS

My brother Ted's story stands out on the positive side of the ledger. We were raised in a Christian home and attended church and Sunday school regularly. When he left home for college, he began to rebel against God. He turned away from the values and standards he had known in his early years. It was during the "hippie" era. He grew long hair, dressed according to the pop-culture role models that reflected his anti-authority attitude. He became involved in attitudes and actions that were dishonoring to God and embarrassing to his family. His parents and family were genuinely concerned and prayed much. They did not become his nagging critics. They were grieved and asked the pastor and church to make him a high prayer priority. He was on the Kent State University campus during the anti-war demonstrations. Through some "divinely appointed" circumstances in life he returned to God. His journey to repentance included seeking forgiveness from God, seeking forgiveness from his family, and seeking forgiveness from his local church. It was nothing short of a miracle.

Today he is a Lieutenant Colonel in the US Army serving as a chaplain. During the Desert Storm conflict he personally led more than twenty men to a saving knowledge of Jesus Christ. I am so proud and thankful for my brother Ted. I am so proud of my parents, sister, brother and a church family that waited, prayed, loved and encouraged a prodigal son who would one day return to his Heavenly Father.

GOD'S PERSPECTIVE

In counseling, one of the primary goals is to assist clients in learning how to maximize their potential and minimize their problems. This is similar to the Christian goal of being conformed to the image of Christ. Christ-likeness results from a lifetime commitment of gradually taking on the characteristics of Christ, of maximizing our full potential in Christ and allowing God's grace to help us deal with our selfish-sinful nature.

"Praise be to the God and Father of our Lord Jesus Christ! In his great mercy he has given us new birth into a living hope through the resurrection of Jesus Christ from the dead, and into an inheritance that can never perish, spoil or fade, kept in heaven for you, who through faith are shielded by God's power until the coming of the salvation that is ready to be revealed in the last time" (1 Peter 1:3-5).

Having been created in the image of God, and being conformed to the likeness of God's Son (see Romans 8:29) is simply a matter of learning to partake of His divine nature. The more we emulate His model the easier it becomes to see ourselves from an eternal perspective, the truest expression of the inner man.

God says WHO we are:
- A royal priesthood
- The elect Children of God
- Heirs of God
- Precious in His sight
- Created in His image
- Blessed with a divine nature

God says WHAT we have:
- a love that can never be understood
- a life that can never die

- a righteousness that can never be tarnished
- a peace that can never be understood
- a rest that can never be disturbed
- a joy that can never be diminished
- a hope that can never be disappointed
- a glory that can never be clouded
- a light that can never be darkened
- a happiness that can never be interrupted
- a strength that can never be enfeebled
- a purity that can never be defiled
- a beauty that can never be marred
- a wisdom that can never be baffled
- resources that can never be exhausted. (Source Unknown)

Are you comfortable now? Ready to have your portrait painted? Probably not entirely yet because it is a learning process. But perhaps you have begun to see why you are so self-conscious about revealing the real you to the world. Now the Master Artist can begin to show you how your portrait is being fashioned with His faithful guidance and steady hand. What an inexpressible blessing: to be His workmanship, to be a portrait in progress.

◆

**The work of the Master Artist is a divinely
orchestrated plan to create His
perfect image in us. We work in a divine-human
cooperative. All our efforts are futile without
his ultimate truth and knowledge of how the painting
should look in the final showing.**

◆

MAKING A MARK

Clifton Fadiman tells a wonderful story about Charles Steinmetz that depicts our dependence upon the Master Artist to know the precise brush-marks necessary to conform us to His remarkable likeness. Charles Steinmetz was a genius of an electrical engineer for General Electric in the early part of the twentieth century. On one occasion after his retirement, when the other engineers around GE were baffled by the breakdown of a complex of machines, they finally asked Steinmetz to come back to see if he could pinpoint the problem. Steinmetz spent several minutes walking around the machines, then took a piece of chalk out of his pocket and made a cross mark on one particular piece of one particular machine.

To their amazement, when the engineers disassembled that particular part of that machine, it turned out to be the precise location of the breakdown.

A few days later, the engineers received a bill from Steinmetz for $10,000 – a staggering sum in those days. This seemed exorbitant, so they returned it to him with a request that he itemize it. After a few more days they received a second, itemized bill:

Making one cross mark: $1.00
Knowing where to put it: $9,999.00 7

That's it! God knows just what it will take—both good times and bad times—to create in us His glorious likeness. And when we experience a breakdown, like the complex machines in the story, our Heavenly Father knows what our need is. When we experience temporary relational, emotional, and spiritual breakdowns, He knows just where to make the supernatural brush-marks on the canvas of our lives. What a wonder!

PERSONAL EVALUATION
&
PRACTICAL APPLICATION

1. Who do you know that best models Christ-like characteristics?

2. What areas in your life need to be more and more conformed to Christ's likeness?

_____

3. Write a "thank you" to significant others who have provided positive role models.

4. Identify one person in your circle of influence to whom you will deliberately "model" Christ-like attitudes and behavior.

5. Can you identify one person in your life who is not a good model? What can you do to avoid the negative influence?

_____
_____
_____
_____

5

THE FOUNDATION

Painting the Background

In the early part of this century many homes were built on wooden blocks or directly on the ground. If they survived after fifty or seventy-five years, they could often be jacked up so that a proper foundation of concrete and steel could be added and the house bolted to it. During earthquakes, floods or other violent natural conditions, those homes that suffer most violently are in mobile home parks, where homes have not been properly anchored to a strong foundation. If the foundation and early influences of your esteem have been negative or based on the pursuit of self or the pleasure of sin, it will create frustration and futility in the search for the real self. If on the other hand your foundation and early influences are positive and biblically based then you will appreciate the work of God in you and see yourself as a masterpiece in the making.

Trouble in almost every area of life can often be traced to a weak or unsteady foundation. Let's look at the importance of foundation through our art student's perspective.

The art student looked at the snapshot and considered the background. A background in art is like the foundation in life. It's supposed to support the subject, not dominate it. What tones should she use that will emphasize those parts of her that she sees are her best characteristics? It can't be too busy. She doesn't want a dark, gloomy background, but neither does she want a

**bright, colorful background that will
overwhelm her image.**
The background and foundation for how we see ourselves
radiate from the wonderful Word of God. God's Word is the foundation upon which our lives are built. The background for our life portrait is systematically and supernaturally intended to draw attention
to our likeness to Christ.

The foundation of your self-image is begun before you are
born and continues throughout your life. Jesus talked about preparing a proper foundation: "Why do you call me, 'Lord, Lord,' and do
not do what I say. I will show you what he is like who comes to me
and hears my words and puts them into practice. He is like a man
building a house, who dug down deep and laid the foundation on
rock. When a flood came, the torrent struck that house but could not
shake it, because it was well built. But the one who hears my words
and does not put them into practice is like a man who built a house
on the ground without a foundation. The moment the torrent struck
that house, it collapsed and its destruction was complete" (Luke
6:46-49).

What can you do if your foundation has been built upon
sand? Of course, to some degree, all of us have issues and events in
our past that have contributed to an unsteady foundation and, thus,
an unbiblical view of self.

The violent 1992-1993 rainstorms in California, and the
infamous El Niño of 1997, took incredible toll on the California
coastline. As late as summer of 1998, people were still watching
their homes slide down eroded hillsides due to unstable foundations.
In the eastern part of Anaheim, homes valued at $400,000 to $1 mil-
lion were threatened, and many were destroyed. The problem
seemed to be the type of soil on which the homes were built, the
amount of hillside that was cut away to construct roads at the base,
and the heavy rainstorms. Had the builders received adequate infor-
mation from geologists about the feasibility of building on these
sites? Most likely not, and lawsuits are still pending.

The Master Artist will create a beautiful you as long as you
submit to the proper foundations of spiritual principles. Let's consid-

er the Foundation Principles, Faith Principles, and Future Principles that will compose the background of your portrait in progress.

FOUNDATION PRINCIPLES

Foundation principles, of course, are those on which we build our life. Charles R. Gerber, in his book *Christ-Centered Self-Esteem,* says that many people build their self-esteem on four foundations: accomplishments, abilities, appearance, and relationship. He goes on to say, "These things will change with age and time. What you can do today strength-wise, you won't be able to do in thirty years."8 Much of what we build our lives on and around, though important and valuable, are finite and terminal. Their value is earth-bound.

Both Peter and Paul talked about who we are and who we can become if we build our lives on the proper foundation, the words of Christ. Peter, in his first epistle, wrote: "You are a chosen people, a royal priesthood, a holy nation, a people belonging to God, that you may declare the praises of him who called you out of darkness into his wonderful light. Once you were not a people, but now you are the people of God; once you had not received mercy, but now you have received mercy" (1 Peter 2:9-10). Paul's words to the saints at Ephesus elaborates on this concept: "You are no longer foreigners and aliens, but fellow citizens with God's people and members of God's household, built on the foundation of the apostles and prophets, with Christ Jesus himself as the chief cornerstone. In him the whole building is joined together and rises to become a holy temple in the Lord" (Ephesians 2:19-21).

There are three ideas in these two passages. First, we are chosen. Second, not only are we chosen, but we are chosen for a purpose: "That you may declare the praises of him who called you out of darkness into his wonderful light." Third, if we are to succeed we need to "join together" with other chosen people, with Jesus as the cornerstone, and rise "to become a holy temple in the Lord."

We Are Chosen. This happened before creation: "He chose us in him before the creation of the world"; and why did He choose us? "To be holy and blameless in his sight. In love he predestined us

59

to be adopted as his sons through Jesus Christ, in accordance with his pleasure and will, to the praise of his glorious grace, which he has freely given us in the One he loves" (Ephesians 1:4-6). Sometimes God allows His chosen ones to go through difficult circumstances as a way to establish or re-establish a strong foundation.

PRESS-BOX WINDOWS TO WASHING WINDOWS
Ron, a successful high school and college athlete, was goal-oriented in his philosophy of life. He eventually became the general manager of a professional football team. He had a good income, was well known in the community and seldom experienced any major distractions from the good life.

Ron was married to a lovely lady who took God and her spiritual life seriously. He was confident of her love and because of his schedule did not invest a lot of focused time in their marriage. His career was the most important thing in his life; it required enormous commitment. Not many years from his retirement, major changes in the front office resulted in his being let go. No problem. He was confident that he would soon be picked up by some other team. Meantime, he would play a little golf and get some rest.

He contacted many decision-makers at various football teams in both leagues, and they all acknowledged his value and offered to do what they could to find him another position. What he thought would be a matter of weeks turned into months, and then years.

During this agonizing time he began to lose his self-esteem and experience serious depression. He lost his appetite. He lost his desire to live. His marriage was stressed. Then his father died. They were close and the loss was great. His dad had always been his confidant.

When Ron called for counseling, he was filled with hopelessness, broken in spirit, and financially stressed. He took a job shuttling and supervising mentally handicapped young people around town as they washed windows at various businesses. He took a job as a janitor, cleaning restrooms. He had literally gone from the peak of success to the valley of despair, from general manager to garbage manager, from press-box windows to washing windows.

Ron knew what it meant to be a Christian, but he was only superficially interested in spiritual things. He would attend church some during the off-season, but was not especially interested in his spiritual development. His foundation for life had centered on what the world had to offer and it was crumbling all around him.

It doesn't take a great deal of imagination to see how Ron's view of self was devastated by life circumstances.

During the course of counseling Ron got on his knees in my office and asked Jesus Christ to forgive him of his sins and become his Savior. It was not long before he began to see life through the filters of faith. He acknowledged that God had allowed much of his suffering in order to bring him to his knees. Then his life began to change. He has returned to professional football and is just a few years away from retirement. He has a renewed appreciation and love for his lovely wife. He has a new appreciation for what is really important in life. He has a passion to tell others of Jesus Christ. As he reviews that disturbing chapter of his life, he understands that, as a chosen one of God, the hard times allowed God to work in his life. He now sees himself as a masterpiece in the making, a portrait in progress, and is taking on the characteristics of Christ, conforming to His image. It is with a radiant smile that He proclaimed,

◆

**"Having the right foundation is
critical in every area of life. But it's absolutely
essential in being able to see yourself as a masterpiece in the making."**

◆

The intent of this story is to emphasize how vulnerable we are when our view of self is exclusively dependent on the world's standards. We can become a masterpiece in the making independent of our vocation, education, or any other yardstick generally considered an indication of success.

We Are Chosen for a Purpose. Our purpose is to glorify God, not ourselves. When we choose accomplishments, abilities, appearance, and relationships as foundations for our life we are attempting to glorify ourselves. How can we change our emphasis from self-centeredness to Christ-centeredness? Paul has one solution: "Whatever is true, whatever is noble, whatever is right, whatever is pure, whatever is lovely, whatever is admirable, if anything is excellent or praiseworthy, think about such things" (Philippians 4:8). At the writing of this book, our president has faced impeachment but has remained in office. Our country continues to debate what is right and wrong. If something is wrong, is it wrong for everyone? And what should be expected from our leaders in terms of personal values and morality? Improper actions seldom result from a one-time impure thought; they come about through allowing improper thoughts to take up residence in the mind. We cannot stop thoughts from entering our minds, but we do not have to let them make their beds there. We must cancel them with true, noble, right, pure, lovely, admirable, excellent, and praiseworthy thoughts.

Knowing and doing the purpose of God in our lives is dependent on cultivating the mind of Christ. We can only fulfill our purpose as we know His purpose for us. **We Need Christian Fellowship.** The third foundational principle in these two passages is that we need to join together with other like-minded people so that, in Christ "the whole building is joined together and rises to become a holy temple in the Lord" (Ephesians 2:19-21). Our self-esteem is strengthened when we fellowship with others who are struggling along with us in this world dominated by the "the ruler of the kingdom of the air, the spirit who is now at work in those who are disobedient" (Ephesians 2:2). It is evident that meeting together to praise God, studying the words of Christ, and praying for each other provides a trusted foundation for growing in Christ.

FAITH PRINCIPLES

The author of the book of Hebrews defines faith as "being sure of what we hope for and certain of what we do not see" (11:1). He then proceeds to list those Old Testament personalities who lived by faith even though they could not see the result of their efforts.

Then in chapter 12 we read these words: "Let us fix our eyes on Jesus, the author and finisher of our faith" (v. 2). Until the end of the chapter the writer exhorts his readers to do those things that will confirm their faith. They are: reflect on your Pardon granted because of Christ; remember your Position in Christ; rejoice in the Power you have in prayer; recommit yourself to God's Purpose for your life; radiate Christ's Peace in your life.

Reflect on the Pardon You Have in Christ. "Blessed is he whose transgressions are forgiven, whose sins are covered. Blessed is the man whose sin the Lord does not count against him and in whose spirit is no deceit" (Psalm 32:1-2; see also Romans 4:7-8). Because of Jesus, God sees you as worthy of His pardon; so worthy, in fact, that He considers you as His child.

I have a friend who was at the very top in his business success. He had the privilege of working with nationally famous people all around the country. He had money, reputation and was well on his way to the good life. Affluence always opens doors that can lead to destruction.

He made illegal business decisions which he later owned up to and subsequently was sentenced to prison for many years. It was this experience that resulted in his building his life purpose on the solid foundation of Jesus Christ and His wonderful Word. His testimony, his re-commitment to Christ, and his true repentance and humility have all worked together to reach many men for Christ in prison. This is what he wrote in a recent letter: "The more God teaches me, the more I need to know Him, the more I feel loved by Him, the more I feel I need his love. He is gracious beyond words, kind beyond measure and truly we can never know the height, depth, length and breadth of his love for us. And yet to be filled to the fullness of Him is all I truly desire. Although I know I will never love Him perfectly as He deserves, I will at least love him whole-heartedly." Though I did not know how he saw himself before his troubles began, I can confidently say that he now sees himself through the eyes of his faithful Heavenly Father; and what a life-changing impact it has had. Although in prison, a new foundation brought him greater freedom than he had ever known in his life.

We do not envy his place in prison but cannot help but be attracted to his intimate and enthusiastic love for God. It took great pain for him to place himself back on the easel of the Master Artist. He is, perhaps for the first time in his life, seeing himself through the eyes of his Savior.

If our foundation is built upon the Rock, the Chief Cornerstone, Jesus Christ our Savior, then the Master Artist can begin to fill in the blank canvas with more background color.

Remember Your Position in Christ. "What is man that you are mindful of him, the son of man that you care for him? You made him a little lower than the angels; you crowned him with glory and honor and put everything under his feet" (Hebrews 2:6-8). The chorus of an old hymn proclaims: "I'm a child of the King, a child of the King: With Jesus my Savior, I'm a child of the King." How magnificently fulfilling to see yourself as a child of the King.

"For you did not receive a spirit that makes you a slave again to fear, but you received the Spirit of sonship. And by him we cry, 'Abba, Father.' The Spirit himself testifies with our spirit that we are God's children. Now if we are children, then we are heirs, heirs of God and co-heirs with Christ" (Romans 8:15-17).

If you believe that you are an heir of God you will conduct your life as the co-heir of Jesus Christ. "Do not conform any longer to the pattern of this world, but be transformed by the renewing of your mind. Then you will be able to test and approve what God's will is—his good, pleasing and perfect will. Do not think of yourself more highly than you ought, but rather think of yourself with sober judgment, in accordance with the measure of faith God has given you" (Romans 12:2-3).

Rejoice in the Power You Have in Prayer. "I tell you the truth, anyone who has faith in me will do what I have been doing. He will do even greater things than these because I am going to the Father. And I will do whatever you ask in my name, so that the Son may bring glory to the Father. You may ask me for anything in my name, and I will do it" (John 14:12-13). Notice the progression: because you are pardoned in Christ, your position is as a child of the King of creation, which gives you great power in your prayers.

Believe it in faith: being sure of what you hope for and certain of what you do not see. In a daily calendar produced by Turning Point Radio Ministries with David Jeremiah, the focus is entirely on prayer. One of the daily quotes by Studdert Kennedy says: "Prayer is not an easy way of getting what we want, but the only way of becoming what God wants us to be."

Recommit Yourself to His Purpose for Your Life. "For we are God's workmanship, created in Christ Jesus to do good works, which God prepared in advance for us to do" (Ephesians 2:10). It is time to be aware of those things God has waiting for you to do, things that have been waiting since you were born. Today, tell your Heavenly Father that you are ready to forget self and concentrate on the wonderful things He has planned for your life. When you begin serving and cooperating with Him then you will be less aware of self and more sensitive to the work of the Savior.

Radiate His Peace in Your Life for His Glory. "Let the peace of Christ rule in your hearts, since as members of one body you were called to peace. And be thankful" (Colossians 3:15). "Peace I leave with you; my peace I give you. I do not give to you as the world gives. Do not let your hearts be troubled and do not be afraid" (John 14:27). Peace is not something that is handed to you; peace is something you earn and learn. The prayer of St. Francis of Assisi, "Lord, make me an instrument of thy peace!" illustrates the work of God in cooperation with our willing obedience.

Our countenance communicates the condition of our hearts. The more like Christ our image becomes, the more our countenance radiates from an inner peace and joy that defies human explanation.

FUTURE PRINCIPLES

Most of us, before we make a major decision such as investing in a home or moving to a new location, will consider all the benefits and challenges of the decision. Following are some benefits that come from a biblical view of self:

- Emotional and personal enrichment
- Freedom to love yourself and others
- Renewed joy and confidence

- Personal achievement
- Inner security
- Patience
- Confidence
- Contentment

Perhaps the greatest challenge in dealing with the "in-progress" dimension of our self-portrait is the required patience. Building on a solid foundation, accepting by faith that God will keep His promise to make me into His image and the confidence to face the future brings our true portrait into clear focus. The strongest antidote for impatience is an unwavering belief that in time it will be as He promised it would be. I believe and I am blessed. Annie Johnson Flint has written:

A father wrote to his son, who was far away from home;
"I have sent you a beautiful gift, It may be delayed, but twill come;
It is what you have wanted most, and have asked for many days;"
And before the child received the gift – he voiced his thanks and praise.

Our Father saith unto us: "Your need shall be supplied;
Ask and receive that your joy be filled, And my joy in you abide."
Shall we wait to thank till we see the answer to every prayer?
Forbear to praise till we feel the lifted pressure of care?
Nay, let us trust His Word and know that the thing is done,
For His promise is just as sure as a father's to his son. 9

PERSONAL EVAUATION
&
PRACTICAL APPLICATION

What kind of a foundation for good self-esteem did your parents, teachers, peers and church build for you? If it wasn't a positive foundation, it's not too late to retrofit that old foundation with new parts. Following are ideas that will give you an image boost.

1. What kind of person are you in your mind's eye? Take a moment and list a few negative things about yourself first:

   _____

   _____

   _____

   Now list positive attributes: (I hope you have to get another piece of paper to hold all the good things about you.)

   _____

   _____

   _____

   Which was easier to do? If making the negative list was easier than the list of positives, how can you strengthen the positive side?

   _____

   _____

   _____

   Have you ever set goals of things you would like to do, places you would like to go, people you would like to meet? Do that now. Be practical, but don't limit your potential. Setting goals can be a real confidence builder.

   _____

   _____

   _____

2. Everyone has some kind of natural talent; maybe you can't think of anything except that you have good handwriting. What are some of your talents, things that you can do better than most people?

_____

_____

_____

3. Who are your friends? Do they encourage or discourage you? Should you drop your friendship with those who puncture your self-esteem? What if you began treating that person or those persons with kindness and consideration? How would they react? List ways you could begin to act positively toward them that might change their reaction to you.

_____

_____

_____

4. How long has it been since you did something special for someone else? Something like taking flowers to a friend. Next week do something especially nice for a different person each day, maybe someone you barely know or who would never expect kindness from you. Work a plan right now.

Monday _____

Tuesday _____

Wednesday _____

Thursday _____

Friday _____

Saturday _____

Sunday _____

5. What are you now dealing with that is a "faith-stretching" challenge? Are you free to stretch? Can you see how this experience will mold you into His image?

6

THE COLORS

Personality Hues

With the background of her portrait
finished, the artist next studied the
colors in her image in the small photo
she would try to reproduce on canvas. Her
face was radiant, her eyes dominant,
framed by dark lashes and eyebrows; red
lips. Her dress was a subtle print of
blues, purples, whites. The sun touched
her dark hair with shades of gold. She
squeezed the various tubes of color onto
her palette and began to transfer the
paint onto the pencil sketch of her face.

The artist in our illustration saw in her photographic image
various flesh tones, black, red, blue, purple, white, and gold. We
often talk in colors. When we feel a little down, we say we are blue;
an aristocrat is a blueblood; someone who is puritanical may be
called a bluenose; the highest award receives a blue ribbon; if we get
angry we see red; when embarrassed we're red-faced; a red flag
symbolizes danger; a red herring is meant to divert attention; a bigot
is a redneck; an inexperienced person is called a greenhorn; green
light means authority to continue; one who is successful in gardening
is said to have a green thumb; a jealous person is beset by the green-
eyed monster; a coward is yellow-bellied; a soldier wounded in battle receives a Purple Heart; someone born to the purple is born into
royalty; witchcraft is called black art; a black cat means bad luck.

When God commissioned Moses to build the Tabernacle it
seems He wanted it to be a contrast to what surrounded His chosen

people at that time. Here they were, wandering around a desolate wilderness, having to be shown where there was water, and having to be fed from heaven. Hot, dry, neutral in color, drab, and mostly lifeless, this was the hopeless land they would be wandering in for forty years. They would need someplace to be renewed, a place where there was hope, a full color, three-dimensional vision of God's promise to come.

"Have them make a sanctuary for me," God told Moses, "and I will dwell among them. Make this tabernacle and all its furnishing exactly like the pattern I will show you" (Exodus 25:8-9). Just prior to these instructions, God had told Moses: "Tell the Israelites to bring me an offering: gold, silver and bronze; blue, purple and scarlet yarn and fine linen; goat hair; ram skins dyed red and hides of sea cows; acacia wood; olive oil for the light; spices for the anointing oil and for the fragrant incense; and onyx stones and other gems" (25:1-7). Colors in abundance for the Tabernacle of the Lord, the model for the future Temple, which Solomon would build.

What do the Tabernacle and Temple and the colors in them have to do with your portrait in progress and with your view of self? Let the New Testament tell you: "We are the temple of the living God. As God has said: 'I will live with them and walk among them, and I will be their God, and they will be my people'" (2 Corinthians 6:16).

Colors often had meaning in Scripture. Isaiah describes God's forgiveness in color: "'Come now, let us reason together,' says the Lord. 'Though your sins are like scarlet, they shall be as white as snow; though they are red as crimson, they shall be like wool'" (Isaiah 1:18). Jesus, at His trial, was draped with a purple robe and crowned with thorns, mocking His claim to be royalty (Mark 15:17). John saw "a throne in heaven with someone sitting on it. And the one who sat there had the appearance of jasper and carnelian. A rainbow, resembling an emerald, encircled the throne. Surrounding the throne were twenty-four other thrones, and seated on them were twenty-four elders. They were dressed in white and had crowns of gold on their heads" (Revelation 4:2-3).

As a way of communicating and illustrating major ingredients in our portrait toward building a strong self-esteem we will include the following colors: flesh tones (Life Purpose); black (Spiritual Warfare); red (Emotions); blue (Challenges); purple (Relationships); white (Forgiveness); gold (Characteristics of Christ).

FLESH TONES DEPICT LIFE PURPOSE

A man or woman without a clearly defined purpose in life is like a ship without a rudder. Each will drift and not drive. Each will end up on the beaches of despair, defeat, and despondency. Purpose in life is a critical dimension in our likeness to Christ.

Why would we choose flesh tones as the color for life purposes? For one thing, skin colors dominate the whole of your body, therefore they are very important colors. Another reason is that the color of your skin does not have to influence your self-image. Skin color has nothing to do with your ability to be successful in whatever you choose, in partnership with God, to do with your life. "Red and yellow, black and white, all are precious in His sight."

John Henry Fabre, the great French naturalist, conducted a most unusual experiment with some processionary caterpillars. (Though I cannot recall the source, I certainly remember the details of the story.) These caterpillars blindly follow the one in front of them. Hence, the name. Fabre carefully arranged them in a circle around the rim of a flowerpot, so that the lead caterpillar actually touched the last one, making a complete circle. In the center of the flowerpot he put pine needles, which is food for the processionary caterpillar. The caterpillars started around this circular flowerpot. Around and around they went, hour after hour, day after day, night after night. For seven full days and seven full nights they went around the flowerpot. Finally, they dropped dead of starvation and exhaustion. With an abundance of food less than six inches away, they literally starved to death.

And much like the processionary caterpillar, people without a well-defined purpose in life, go in circles, following others in the relentless pursuit of self. They just keep doing what comes naturally and never come to the knowledge that the Creator God has a plan to re-create His image in them. If they never are able to see themselves and their life purpose from His perspective then they too often become exhausted and spiritually starved.

◆

Knowing where you want to go in life requires a plan. Well-defined goals, both short term and long term are an integral part of your life portrait.

◆

The following principles of success have been emphasized in countless books. They are not new; they have been around for thousands of years. God thought of them first.

- **Cultivate a Healthy Positive Attitude.** When you know where you want to go you can be assured "that in all things God works for the good of those who love him, who have been called according to his purpose" (Romans 8:28). Being called "according to his purpose" means that God knew you were going to be His long before you were born. God wants you to succeed. There are only two requirements: (1) love God; (2) be sure you have surrendered to "his purpose."

  Cultivating a positive, purposeful attitude about life and living is really another way of saying, "cultivating a biblical attitude." It means that I am deliberately willing to determine to grow in the likeness of Christ.

  It is so sad to counsel with someone who has cultivated a negative attitude about life in general and self in particular. A negative attitude is graphically depicted in the countenance of a person. Their negative view of self is frequently a symptom of heart problems. Their extensive list of what is wrong in the church, home, and workplace is simply an indication of the pain that is within.

  By God's grace and His promised provision – commit yourself to cooperate with God as He brushes a positive, biblical attitude onto the canvas of your life-portrait.

- **Define Your Purpose.** "Forgetting what is behind and straining toward what is ahead, press on toward the goal to win the prize

72

for which God has called you" (Philippians 3:13-14). Never replay the old tapes of failure or discouragement of the past that will distort your opinion of yourself, your abilities, and your trust that God will work alongside you. Strain and press on toward your goal. Our purpose in life is to be conformed to the image of Christ. Once we acknowledge our ultimate purpose in life we are free to fulfill our many life purposes with enthusiasm and satisfaction.

• **Go the Extra Mile.** "If someone forces you to go one mile, go with him two miles" (Matthew 5:41). No one has ever achieved his goal without being willing to do more than what was expected of him. On the way to work a couple of days ago I saw a bumper sticker that read: "It is all about me." Cultivating a selfless attitude and going beyond what is expected is one of the noticed features of a Christ-like portrait. In the midst of a self-dominated society, selflessness is a remarkable personal trait.

• **Live Life Enthusiastically.** Not only does it build your self-esteem, it delights the one you are doing it for. "Whatever your hand finds to do, do it with all your might" (Ecclesiastes 9:10). The word enthusiasm in Greek is a combination of two words: "en" meaning in, and "theos" meaning God. Enthusiasm means being inspired by God. I have never been accused of lacking in enthusiasm about life and ministry. The Master Artist has continually painted this feature into my life portrait. However, from time to time I really get discouraged. With a personality like mine – when I am discouraged – I might as well carry around a large sign announcing it. I have always marveled how the Lord Jesus will send someone alongside of me during these times. Enthusiasm is contagious. Their love for me, zeal for God, and excitement about life significantly influences my perspective in life. It's like going to a spiritual chiropractor to get a perspective adjustment. There is nothing like a good dose of enthusiasm to create a radiant countenance.

• **Practice the Ministry Principle.** "Let us not give up meeting together, as some are in the habit of doing, but let us encourage one another" (Hebrews 10:25). We need the encouragement and input of others whom we can respect and trust. We are often told in Scripture to pray for each other, encourage one another daily, rejoice together, confess our faults to one another. We need the strength of others to help us achieve our purposes. Those who have developed good relational skills are blessed indeed. It seems our churches have many people with great needs. In fact, people often choose which church they will attend by how much it promises to do for them. In order to have the features of Christ in our portrait we must be ever increasingly sensitive to the needs of others. There is no greater biblical paradox.

◆

**It is in giving that I gain. It is in serving that I grow.
It is in caring for others that I am nurtured.**

◆

When I deal with individuals in counseling who are depressed I generally encourage them to begin caring for the needs of others. It is quite amazing what happens when we change the focus from our deficits to the painful needs of others. It's Christ-like!

- **Maintain Sound Physical Health.** "Do you not know that your body is a temple of the Holy Spirit, who is in you, whom you have received from God? Therefore honor God with your body" (1 Corinthians 6:19-20). Taking care of our bodies is an essential ingredient in completing our masterpiece. Taking care of our bodies is a spiritual stewardship. Many physical problems are clearly outside of our human control. The discipline required to take good care of yourself physically promotes discipline in every area of your life. Good stewardship of your body pays remarkable dividends and is pleasing to your heavenly Father.

- **Think Accurately.** "Do not conform any longer to the pattern of this world, but be transformed by the renewing of your mind. Then you will be able to test and approve what God's will is— his good, pleasing and perfect will" (Romans 12:2). You renew your mind by learning, whether you learn more about your goal or learn more about your God. You cannot think accurately unless you know what is accurate. The Bible tells what we should think about and warns us to avoid certain thoughts. How a person thinks is perhaps a personal trait that is more difficult to see on the canvas of your portrait in progress. The more my mind, imagination, and thoughts are conformed to the mind of Christ – the more my behavior reflects His purposes.

- **Maintain Self-Discipline.** "Run in such a way as to get the prize. Everyone who competes in the games goes into strict training. They do it to get a crown that will not last; but we do it to get a crown that will last forever. Therefore I do not run like a man running aimlessly; I do not fight like a man beating the air. No, I beat my body and make it my slave so that after I have preached to others, I myself will not be disqualified for the prize" (1 Corinthians 9:24-27). We hear too frequently about well-known religious leaders who diminished their effectiveness because they did not "practice what they preached." This caution is not reserved for preachers; it applies to anyone who proclaims the name of Christ. Self-discipline is a minute-by-minute exercise. The Evil One is always alert to any chink in our armor.

- **Keep the Faith.** "The Lord your God has given you the land. Go up and take possession of it as the Lord, the God of your father, told you. Do not be afraid; do not be discouraged" (Deuteronomy 1:21). Sometimes it is necessary to give ourselves pep talks when we feel discouraged -- it works! Try it. True faith shines brightest on the face of a believer when they are facing the unknown or things that are outside their control.

- **Learn from Defeat.** "For though a righteous man falls seven times, he rises again" (Proverbs 24:16). Others will forget your defeats more quickly than you will. Do not dwell on them -- learn from them.

- **Budget Time.** "Be very careful, then, how you live, not as unwise but as wise, making the most of every opportunity" (Ephesians 5:15-16).

Do not allow these many important personal and spiritual traits to overwhelm you. Keep in mind that being conformed to the image of Christ is a lifetime process. These brush marks on the canvas of your life will eventually be radiant in its color and clear in its presentation. God has promised, with your faithful cooperation, to paint His character in you.

BLACK DEPICTS SPIRITUAL WARFARE

Today our society seems fascinated with the "spiritual" world. Everything from television shows about witches, the supernatural, and vampires to movies depicting witch explorations and communications with the dead demonstrate our present preoccupation with a world and powers that are unseen. Although these powers may be unseen, they are real and active.

Jesus warned His disciples about the thief who "comes only to steal and kill and destroy" (John 10:10). Charles R. Gerber, in his book *Christ-Centered Self-Esteem*, tells why Satan likes low self-esteem. "The major reason is that low self-esteem becomes a stronghold that he will use to kill, steal and destroy (John 10:10). Paul discusses 'strongholds' in 2 Corinthians 10:4. The Greek word for stronghold used here is *ochuroma*. It means 'to make firm, fortress.' Low self-esteem becomes a fortress from which he can operate. Jesus talked about one of Satan's techniques. Before you can rob a person you must first tie up the person who will be robbed (Matt. 12:29). Being tied up can be one of the consequences of low esteem. The stronghold of low esteem has two elements: 1. the person feels guilty for the wasted potential. They feel guilty for what they are not doing with their life; and 2. the person feels embarrassed for who they are or the way they look. Self-criticism is frequently a sign of #2."[10]

Part of our service to our Lord is to evangelize. This takes boldness, and if your self-esteem is low, you cannot be bold. All the while the Adversary gloats at his success.

The Evil One uses everything he can to get to our spirits. Jack Hayford, in his book *Taking Hold of Tomorrow*, tells about an incident when he was ministering at a conference in Oregon. A young woman asked for prayer because she was having horrible nightmares. Pastor Hayford felt led to ask her what she had on her bedroom walls. The young woman was startled by the question, but after a minute she replied that she had a poster she had bought at a rock concert on which were skulls, snakes, crudity, and general symbols of evil. She went on to explain that the poster was at her home but she continued to have nightmares even though she had been staying more than two hundred miles from her home.

Pastor Jack explained, "That makes no difference. You submitted yourself to something evil and time and space make no difference in the spiritual realm." He then asked her what she wanted to do. "I want to get rid of it – I really do." Pastor Hayford knew she meant getting rid of more than the poster, she wanted to be rid of the mental and spiritual anguish of this spiritual warfare. He prayed for the young woman, rebuking the power of darkness that infested her home and her mind. He then asked the girl if anyone was at her home now. The girl responded that her mother was. The pastor suggested that she call her mother and have her tear the poster off the wall and burn it – now! The mother did and two days later when they met in the dining hall she said, "For the first time in a month –two nights – no nightmares!"[11]

Paul tells us to put on the full armor of God against the powers of evil. He reminds us that our war is not in a conventional sense – but with spiritual wickedness. At the sign of triumph Satan's host doth flee;

On, then, Christian soldiers, on to victory!
Hell's foundations quiver at the shout of praise;
Brothers, lift your voices, loud your anthems raise!
Onward Christian soldiers, marching as to war,
With the cross of Jesus, going on before.[12]

RED DEPICTS EMOTIONS

When I meet a person for the initial counseling session I can tell a lot about their level of pain by their countenance. Emotions always manifest themselves in a person's face. In our Lay Counselor Training class we ask our students to use a mirror and attempt to depict various emotions in their countenance. What does anger look like? What does genuine joy look like? Are you able to see the unique features on the face of someone who is in love? The students begin to understand how critical it is for an effective counselor to be able to read the messages of a person's countenance.

I can well remember a Christian lady who came to me for counseling. When I met her in the waiting room I immediately noticed her angry, bitter eyes. After being with her for just a short time I began to understand how her painful life circumstances had so deeply wounded her. Her bitterness had contributed to poor physical health, spiritual anemia, and relational deficits.

On the other hand, positive emotions are health producing and contagious. Can you picture in your mind's imagination what a person looks like that is truly joy-filled?

◆

Guilt, anger, jealousy, excessive sensitivity, hatred, worry, anxiety, depression, and many other negative emotions are exaggerated if you have a low self-esteem.

◆

When you are not confident of your own abilities or position you tend to resent anyone who appears to recognize your weaknesses. This resentment contributes to unmanaged emotions.

Dr. James Dobson says about emotions: "Emotions must always be accountable to the faculties of reason and will. That accountability is doubly important for those of us who purport to be Christians. When we experience defeat during life's spiritual pilgrimage, it is likely that negative emotions will play a dominant role in that discouragement. Satan is devastatingly effective in using the weapons of guilt, rejection, fear, embarrassment, grief, depression, loneliness and misunderstanding. Indeed, human beings are vulnerable creatures who could not withstand these satanic pressures without divine assistance."[13]

Paul talks about emotions as if they were garments that, if negative, you must rid yourself of and, if positive, you must clothe yourself with. Then he says to "let the peace of Christ rule in your hearts, since as members of one body you were called to peace" (Colossians 3:8, 12, 15).

What the Bible refers to as the Fruit of the Spirit provides specific goals for emotional and spiritual growth. Imagine a portrait that radiates love, joy, peace, longsuffering, kindness, goodness, faithfulness, gentleness, and self-control.

BLUE DEPICTS CHALLENGES

Because a blue ribbon signifies a winner, we will consider blue as the color to represent difficult life challenges. If we spend our lives "playing it safe" and never strive for a goal we will never know what it is like to be first-class, a winner, the best in the field. What does it take to meet a challenge? It takes faith! Hebrews 11 talks about the people of the Old Testament who were all blue-ribbon winners: Noah built an ark in a desert place by faith and survived a great flood. Abraham left his lifetime home and traveled to a strange land where people practiced strange rituals and spoke a strange language, yet he became the father of a great nation, God's chosen people. Moses refused to conform to his Egyptian stepmother's ways and eventually led six hundred thousand men plus women, children, and people of other races into the Promised Land. These people who are now with God are described by the writer of Hebrews as "a great cloud of witnesses" surrounding us, cheering us on, encouraging us to accept challenges, to strive for the blue ribbon, to be winners.

The solution begins with changing the way we react to what has been programmed into our minds. William J. Diehm says that overcoming a problem is like programming a computer. Where programming a computer involves following a proper sequence, programming our minds is done with godly repetition. "Just keep pushing the good buttons until they take over, and most of the problems of life can be handled automatically. (1) Accept people and life as they are, not as you think they should be. (2) Don't establish blame. What difference does it make whose fault it is? Solve the problem. (3) Be content with what you have and then get more. (4) Get excited about playing the game of life. Enjoy being blocked, hit, tackled, and knocked down. That's part of the game. (5) Refuse to take more off the conveyor belt of life than you are able. (6) Don't let the past wreck you. Deep-freeze your bad memories. (7) Turn impossible problems over to God and leave them there. (8) Don't forget the 'Fun button' to recharge your batteries. Everyone needs rest, diversion, change of pace and recreation. (9) The Greek word *katallagete* means 'be reconciled to God' and implies 'be a close friend with God.'"[14]

PURPLE DEPICTS RELATIONSHIPS

Purple is the color of royalty; we use it to describe relationships. We are children of the King: "How great is the love the Father has lavished on us, that we should be called children of God!" (1 John 3:1). The children of Britain's royalty are constantly being watched by the world, and sometimes judged unfairly because of bad press. Just so, the children of the King are constantly being watched and often judged unfairly. What does this have to do with self-esteem? The way we treat those with whom we have relationships will either build up or tear down our self-esteem. Jesus' admonition to "love your neighbor as yourself" (Mark 12:31) means that you will treat your neighbor the way you treat yourself. If you do not like yourself you are not going to treat yourself or your neighbor well.

The Bible tells us many things about our relationships:

- **Between children and parents:** "Children, obey your parents in the Lord, for this is right. 'Honor your father and mother'— which is the first commandment with a promise'—that it may go well with you and that you may enjoy long life on the earth.' Fathers, do not exasperate your children; instead, bring them up in the training and instruction of the Lord" (Ephesians 6:1-4).
- **Between husbands and wives:** "Wives, submit [subject yourself] to your husbands as to the Lord. Husbands, love your wives, just as Christ loved the church and gave himself up for her" (Ephesians 5:22, 25).
- **Between brothers and sisters in Christ:** "Submit [subject yourself] to one another out of reverence for Christ" (Ephesians 5:21).
- **Between servant and master:** "Slaves [servants, employees], obey your earthly masters with respect and fear, and with sincerity of heart, just as you would obey Christ. And masters, treat

your slaves in the same way. Do not threaten them, since you know that he who is both their Master and yours is in heaven, and there is no favoritism with him" (Ephesians 6:5,9).

- **Toward governing authorities:** "Everyone must submit himself to the governing authorities, for there is no authority except that which God has established. Consequently, he who rebels against the authority is rebelling against what God has instituted, and those who do so will bring judgment on themselves" (Romans 13:1-2).

- **Toward everybody else:** "Lord, who may dwell in your sanctuary? Who may live on your holy hill? He whose walk is blameless and who does what is righteous, who speaks the truth from his heart and has no slander on his tongue; who does his neighbor no wrong and casts no slur on his fellow man, who despises a vile man but honors those who fear the Lord, who keeps his oath even when it hurts, who lends his money without usury and does not accept a bribe against the innocent. He who does these things will never be shaken" (Psalm 15).

WHITE DEPICTS FORGIVENESS

Forgiveness is one of the core features of the heart of God. For God so loved the world – He forgave us of our sins. From cover to cover the Bible emphasizes the importance of giving and receiving forgiveness. Forgiveness is essential in our portrait in progress. The absence of a forgiving spirit will be a readily noticed blemish.

The cycle of forgiveness often has to start with forgiving yourself. My daughter Kara expresses this concept in this special way:

---◆---

"Forgiveness isn't to free those who hurt you but to free you from the hurt."

---◆---

Why is forgiving so hard? Because we tend to believe certain myths about "forgiving." Somehow, like bad genes, these sincere but misguided notions get passed down from one generation to another. It is similar to the not-so-biblical but very familiar statement: "God helps those who help themselves." It seems right and is certainly familiar, but it is only a myth or misconception of how God works with us.

The most prevalent myths about forgiveness to which we fall victim could be labeled:

- **Hypocrite Myth:** I can't forgive her yet because I don't feel like it, and I don't want to be a hypocrite.
- **Unforgivable myth:** What he did to me is so awful that it's unforgivable.
- **Memory Myth:** I'll never forget the awfulness and hurt of what she did to me, so I probably haven't truly forgiven her.
- **Revenge Myth:** I can't forgive him until I get even. When I'm deeply wounded by someone, it's only fair that he should also suffer in some way.
- **Restoration Myth:** I will never be the same or regain what I have lost. The wounds are too deep.
- **Reconciliation Myth:** Biblical forgiveness requires that I reconcile with her, but I don't want anything to do with her. No way! She hasn't changed at all.

Some sincere, godly people truly believe these myths or misconceptions when they are responding to the situation through the filters of emotional pain. Pain makes it difficult to see God's truth clearly and we become vulnerable to misconceptions of genuine forgiveness.

In his book *Caring Enough to Forgive*, David Augsburger lists five steps to restoring my relationship to the offender:

Step 1: Forgive by realizing wrongdoing. You have been hurt. Harboring unforgiveness is wrong; it may "pay back" the person who hurt you, but it definitely injures your own body, mind, and spirit, diminishing your own sense of self-worth.

Step 2: Forgive by reaffirming love. This means that, first, you stop devaluing the offending person; second, recognize that this person is also precious in God's eyes. He created him, He loves him, He forgives him, He wants him to experience the joy of salvation.

82

God's commandment is, "Love each other as I have loved you" (John 15:12), not because you feel like it but because God loved you first and expects you to pass it on to your enemies as well as your friends.

Step 3: Forgive by releasing the past. Augsburger says that "painful experiences must be accepted emotionally as well as rationally. When the shock of an experience evokes more pain than can be accepted and assimilated at the moment of impact, then the emotional processing will follow, sometimes days later. This grieving and regrieving is a way of absorbing the full impact of what has occurred and coming to believe it with the heart as well as the head. When the loss is immense, as in the death of a person or the loss of a relationship or the rejection of love, months and sometimes years of mourning may be required before the loss is accepted emotionally. The heart has a memory too, and it must be allowed to feel its pain fully before releasing its hold on the past."15

Step 4: Forgive by renewing repentance. "Repentance is a turning, a turning from and turning to. In repenting, one turns from what was without denying or ignoring what has been; and one turns to what can be by choosing new ways of being and behaving."16

Step 5: Forgive by rediscovering community. "Creating, sustaining, celebrating community is costly. It requires the sacrifice of self-denial and of the civilizing force of avoidance. In community, persons are included not ignored; invited to explore relationships, not overlooked and evaded when they provoke tensions or exaggerate uncomfortable differences."17

GOLD DEPICTS SPIRITUAL GROWTH

There is something exhilarating and self-esteem building about making a commitment to win the prize, to attain the crown, and to complete the race. One of the most dangerous attitudes in our spiritual journey is what I refer to as "auto-pilot" living. A commitment to maintain or just get by is so empty and unsatisfying.

Go for the gold! How often do we hear that during the Olympics? In Paul's day it was a crown, and it was not gold: "Do you not know that in a race all the runners run, but only one gets the prize? Run in such a way as to get the prize. Everyone who competes in the games goes into strict training. They do it to get a crown that will not last; but we do it to get a crown that will last forever. Therefore I do not run like a man running aimlessly; I do not fight like a man beating the air. No, I beat my body and make it my slave so that after I have preached to others, I myself will not be disqualified for the prize" (1 Corinthians 9:24-27).

You do not compete with other Christians for the imperishable crown; you compete against the Evil One who is fighting to regain your soul. One way he does it is by distorting your thinking so that you devalue God's great creation—YOU! Paul says, "I beat my body and make it my slave." He lived as though he were in training, preparing to fight a great fight or run a winning race. He asks the Galatians: "You were running a good race. Who cut in on you and kept you from obeying the truth? That kind of persuasion does not come from the one who calls you" (Galatians 5:7-8).

Approaching all of life with the idea that you are a portrait in progress will allow you to pursue the "prize for which God has called [you] heavenward in Christ Jesus" (Philippians 3:14). You must pursue those characteristics, in cooperation with the Master Artist, that will make significant brush marks on the canvas of your life. Determination to work with God in being conformed to His image requires an unswerving, laser sharp focus on the goal in spite of difficulties and doubts.

COURAGE TO COMPLETE

In the 1986 New York City Marathon, almost twenty thousand runners entered this famous race. What is memorable about it is not who won, but who finished last. His name is Bob Wieland. He finished 19, 413th. Dead last. Bob completed the New York Marathon in – are you ready for this? – four days, two hours, forty-eight minutes, seventeen seconds. Unquestionably the slowest marathon in history. Ever.

What makes Wieland's story so special? Bob ran with his arms. Seventeen years earlier, when he was a soldier serving in Vietnam, Bob's legs were blown off in battle. When he runs,

Wieland sits on a fifteen-pound "saddle" and covers his fists with pads. He "runs" with his arms. Bob ran with determination and endurance. He refused to allow the limitations of his physical life to rob him of the pure joy of fulfilling his lifetime dream.[18]

God will provide the courage and the energy to complete the process of becoming like Him, regardless of our limitations in life.

◆

**"His divine power has given us everything we
need for life and godliness through
our knowledge of him who called us by his own glory and goodness.
Through these he has given us his very great and precious promises,
so that through them you may participate in the
divine nature and escape the corruption in this
world caused by evil desires."
II Peter 1: 3-4**

◆

PERSONAL EVALUATON
&
PRACTICAL APPLICATION

1. Each personality contains unique colors. Take a moment and make a list of colors that can be found in your portrait. As you list these, determine if these are true colors of your portrait, colors that are seen through the Master's eyes.

_____

_____

_____

2. Do you ever feel like the processionary caterpillar mentioned in the chapter? Do you have well-defined goals, both short term and long term?   List them.
Short term:

_____

_____

_____

Long term:

_____

_____

_____

3. Take a moment to reflect on the following principles of success in your goals.

    • Cultivate a Healthy Positive Attitude
    • Define Your Purpose
    • Go the Extra Mile
    • Live Life Enthusiastically
    • Practice the Ministry Principle
    • Maintain Sound Physical Health
    • Think Accurately
    • Maintain Self-Discipline
    • Keep the Faith

- Learn From Defeat
- Budget Time

4. How does a person cultivate a positive and pleasing attitude? Can you identify "attitudes" in your life that are harmful to you or others?

5. Learning how to "Practice the Ministry Principle" is one of the most important aspects of growing in Christ. During the next month, pray about, prepare for, and practice the ministry principle. List several things you personally can do or are doing to minister to others.

_____

_____

_____

THE PORTRAIT

Analyzing the Near-Finished Project

A young boy walked into a small neighborhood grocery store and stopped at a public telephone. The owner of the store watched the boy as he dialed a number. The grocer heard him say, "Hello, Dr. London. Do you want to hire a boy to cut the grass and run errands for you? Oh, you already have a boy! Are you happy with the boy you have? Okay, then, good-bye doctor."

As the boy turned to leave the store the owner said, "Just a minute, son. If you're looking for work, I could use a boy like you."

"Thank you, sir, but I have a job," the boy replied.

"But I just heard you trying to get a job from Dr. London."

"No, sir," said the boy, "I already work for Dr. London. I was just checking up on how I'm doing."

This humorous and insightful story brings us to the point of this chapter: checking up on how we are doing in seeing ourselves as a portrait in progress, as a masterpiece in the making.

The list is unending of spiritual and personal traits that reflect the image of Christ, but there are several that are at the core of the renewing process. Without these fundamental ingredients the portrait will not be complete in its likeness to the Master.

The artist put her brushes and palette aside, stood up, and looked down at her portrait. She was a little startled; it was almost like looking in a mirror. No, it was different. There was more—what was it? Sparkle? Assurance? She felt tears fill her eyes. The image she saw was breathtakingly beautiful – it was a reflection of the person she wanted to be.

The professor stood behind her and placed his hand on her shoulder.

The very essence of being a portrait in progress means it is incomplete. We will never be finally complete until we are with Christ. However, at any given time in life we can pause to analyze how we are doing compared to the ultimate portrait – the image of Christ.

It is time now to analyze your self-portrait and see how you are doing. We will do this by comparing your portrait in progress with the teaching you have received from the Master Artist. God, the Master Artist, was completely satisfied with His original creation before the Evil One stepped in and damaged His perfect work. God sent His Son to teach us how the damage that was done could be repaired. At the end of His time on earth, teaching and showing by example what perfection was, Jesus tried to prepare His disciples for His death. He gave them a new commandment: "Love one another. As I have loved you, so you must love one another" (John 13:34).

The Apostle Paul picked up on this in 1 Corinthians 13:13 by describing how love behaves toward others. When we can get to the place where the way we treat others is more important than the way they treat us, we are on the way to achieving a biblical self-image. At the end of his description of love, Paul then says: "And now these three remain: faith, hope and love. But the greatest of these is love." We will use these three checkpoints to analyze your personal portrait in progress: faith, (which is **Courage**,) hope (which is **Confidence**,) and love (which is **Compassion**).

COURAGE: FAITH IN ACTION

When we reflect on the heroes of faith listed in Hebrews 11, we are impressed that even though their accomplishments for God varied, the one obvious common denominator was a faith-saturated determination. They were men and women of incredible courage.

Cervantes said, "He who loses wealth loses much; he who

90

loses a friend loses more; but he who loses courage loses everything. To weary of life is to walk into an emotional 'badlands' where desperados of black emotion may ambush you at any turn."[19]

One of Satan's prime weapons is discouragement. He does his best to rob us of our faith in God and our faith in the power that God gives us. Ephesians 6:10-18 describes in detail the tremendous power struggle going on in our war against spiritual forces. The chapter explodes with encouraging instructions on how to "take your stand against the devil's schemes. For our struggle is not against flesh and blood, but against the rulers, against the authorities, against the powers of this dark world and against the spiritual forces of evil in the heavenly realms. Put on the full armor of God, so that you may be able to stand your ground." In this way we will "be strong in the Lord and in his mighty power."

As I write this book I read in newspapers and magazines, and in brochures from banks, insurance companies, utility companies, and hear on the radio and television the fearful uncertainties about the transition into the new millenium. This is the consequence of living in an electronic age. Survivalists are sounding advice on getting a gun and heading to the hills before someone robs you of your hoarded supplies of water and food. Respected organizations such as AARP suggested that we "prepare for the possibility (even if it's remote) of a power outage. Have extra food and bottled water on hand. Fill up the heating oil tank. Think carefully before booking overseas travel for early January 2000. Keep paper records of bank deposits, credit-card and mortgage payments and other financial transactions for several months leading up to Jan. 1, 2000. Have enough cash on hand to get through a long holiday weekend."[20] What's a believer to do surrounded by so many fear-saturated circumstances? One author refers to these fear-causing situations in our lives as the "malignant disease of the what-ifs."

Commit yourself to cultivate a growing sense of spiritual courage. Having courage doesn't mean you should ignore the warnings and words of advice regarding Y2K. A wise person will take the advice of those who have our best interest in mind and prepare for possible interruptions in the normal conveniences we have become used to. Just as you would prepare for the possibility of any natural disaster, such as storms, you should take sensible precautions. But this does not mean you run off and hide, clutching your belongings as though there was no hope. Courage is grown to its fullest capacity when in the midst of difficult circumstances.

Charles Colson in his book, *Loving God*, tells the story of a fourth-century Christian who lived in a remote village, tending his garden and spending much of his time in prayer. One day he thought he heard the voice of God telling him to go to Rome, so he obeyed, setting out on foot. Weary weeks later, he arrived in the city at the time of a great festival. The little monk followed the crowd surging down the streets into the Coliseum. He saw the gladiators stand before the emperor and say, "We who are about to die salute you." Then he realized these men were going to fight to the death for the entertainment of the crowd. He cried out, "In the name of Christ, stop!"

As the games began, he pushed his way through the crowd, climbed over the wall, and dropped to the floor of the arena. When the crowd saw this tiny figure rushing to the gladiators and saying, "In the name of Christ, stop!" They thought it was part of the show and began laughing.

When they realized it wasn't, the laughter turned to anger. As he was pleading with the gladiators to stop, one of them plunged a sword into his body. He fell to the sand. As he was dying, his last words were, "In the name of Christ, stop!"

Then a strange thing happened. The gladiators stood looking at the tiny figure lying there. A hush fell over the Coliseum. High in the upper rows, a man stood and made his way to the exit. Others began to follow. In dead silence, everyone left the Coliseum.

The year was 391 BC, and that was the last battle to the death between gladiators in the Roman Coliseum. Never again in the great stadium did men kill each other for the entertainment of the crowd, all because of one tiny voice that could hardly be heard above the tumult. One courageous voice – one life – that spoke the truth in God's name.

◆

Faith will quiet your feelings of insecurity and inadequacy as you look to Him for wisdom and courage.

◆

Having faith in God's plan and purpose for your life will make a difference in how you see yourself and will add vibrant color qualities to the Master Artist's portrait in progress.

FEAR OR FAITH

Chuck and Loretta Emert have been partners in marriage and ministry for forty-five years. They have invested in Christian Heritage College for the last twelve years. They have participated in short-term missionary ministry in many foreign countries. Chuck was one of the most popular and loved professors in the entire college. Students constantly expressed their love for his teaching and especially for their life of faith. It was with some considerable difficulty that they accepted God's clear call to full-time missionary work in Romania. It was sad for the Christian Heritage family to think about their leaving.

Shortly after announcing their intentions to go into full-time missions ministry Chuck was diagnosed with prostate cancer. Now what? They determined they would do all they could to get good medical attention and follow through with their plans to go to Romania. Within weeks of their faith-saturated and courageous decision to go – Loretta was diagnosed with breast cancer. Now what? You talk about a faith-stretching experience! After seeking medical advice and treatment they unanimously concluded that God had called them and would provide for their needs – including strength and courage to serve God on the mission field, a courage that demands confidence in the Master.

They are serving God in Romania and are "living testimonies" of human courage and genuine faith. No cancer exists in either of them. They are strong, healthy, and enthusiastic about serving God.

CONFIDENCE: HOPE IN ACTION

About five years ago, Christian social critic Richard John Neuhaus was being driven from the Pittsburgh airport to a speaking engagement. During the drive, one of his hosts persisted in decrying the disintegration of the American social fabric and the disappearance of Christian values from our culture. Cases in point were too numerous to mention, but Pastor Neuhaus's host tried anyway. After the tedious drive, Neuhaus offered these words of advice: "The times may be bad, but they are the only times we are given. Remember, hope is still a Christian virtue, and despair is a mortal sin."21

If you have hope you can become confident. The word for hope in the Greek language means "confident expectation." Instead of focusing on my liabilities I will become confident in what God is doing in and through me. "Hope does not disappoint us, because God has poured out his love into our hearts by the Holy Spirit, whom he has given us" (Romans 5:5).

God, the Master Artist, will give me a whole new sense of confidence that He is working on my behalf. The genuine test of my value must be based upon the promises of God. My hope is built on His faithfulness. Cultivating a sense of hope (confident expectations) makes it impossible for me to be manipulated by self-doubt or self-conscious feelings of insecurity or inadequacy.

- I am confident that God will take care of me: "Cast all your anxiety on him because he cares for you" (1 Peter 5:7).
- I am confident that I will be able to do all He knows I can do: "I can do everything through him who gives me strength" (Philippians 4:13).
- I am confident that God is interested in me and confident in His ability to work through me. Paul showed that his confidence was based on his trust in the Lord

Jesus: "Being confident of this, that he [the Master Artist] who began a good work in you will carry it on to completion until the day of Christ Jesus" (Philippians 1:6).

Author Bruce Larson gives a personal description of confidence. "On his twentieth birthday, our youngest son bought himself his first ten-speed bicycle with a tax refund from the Internal

Revenue Service. The day after he bought his new bike, an all-Florida professional bike race was held in our town. Mark, along with two friends, decided to enter. I tried to discourage him. I told him bike racing was very sophisticated and he was foolish to try it with no training. 'But it will be a good experience,' he said.

"He returned that night with the first-place cup. Needless to say, we were astounded. I asked him what happened. 'Well,' he said, 'I know long distance bike racing is very tricky. You have to learn to pace yourself carefully and make your move at the right time. Since I didn't know exactly what to do, I just started out pedaling as fast as I could and nobody ever passed me.'"22 Now, that's confidence!

In every important endeavor in life the dynamic of hope is the single most powerful influence. Hopelessness is devastating. Hopelessness is defeating. Hopelessness erodes motivation. Hopelessness is used by Satan to cause despair.

On the contrary, hope is the single most important source of motivation when dealing with the extraordinary challenges of life.
- Hope promotes endurance.
- Hope produces courage.
- Hope provides health.
- Hope prevails in hard times.
- Hope promises life beyond the pain.
- Hope protects from the paralysis of despair.

There's just nothing like a good dose of hope to enhance the radiance of your portrait in progress. Glory!

In his first epistle, John summed up confidence and introduced us to our next point (compassion): "Dear friends, if our hearts do not condemn us, we have confidence before God and receive from him anything we ask, because we obey his commands and do what pleases him. And this is his command: to believe in the name of his Son, Jesus Christ, and to love one another as he commanded us" (1 John 3:21-23).

COMPASSION: LOVE IN ACTION
If you want others to see Christ in you, commit yourself to deliberately and consistently cultivate the quality of love in your

heart and life. Supernatural, selfless love is always a prominent feature on a portrait completed by the Master Artist.

As Paul did in 1 Corinthians 13, we have saved the very best until last. "But the greatest of these is love." The world's view of love is temporary and unfulfilling. Many times it is selfish, conditional, and demanding. But God views love differently. Love means many things, but in this section we want to show how the emotion of love expresses itself in a tangible way as compassion. The words "I love you" reflect the intent of the heart. But there is no credit for good intentions. Love that makes a difference is best demonstrated by God's great love. He said, " I love you and because of my love for you I will send my only Son to die for you and pay the penalty for sin in your behalf." Because of His love you can have life eternal and life more abundant. What love!

An expert in the law of Moses wanted to test Jesus to see if he could find something to accuse Him of. So he asked Jesus, "Teacher, what must I do to inherit eternal life?" Jesus asked him what the law said. The expert, probably picking up on what Jesus had preached earlier, replied, " 'Love the Lord your God with all your heart and with all your soul and with all your strength and with all your mind,' and, 'Love your neighbor as yourself.' " Jesus agreed and told him to do this. But the lawyer was not satisfied with this answer. "And who is my neighbor?" he pressed.

Jesus then proceeded to give the parable of the good Samaritan. You know the story about the Jewish man going from Jerusalem to Jericho when he was attacked by robbers and beaten badly and left for dead; neither a priest nor a Levite, the "good" Jews, stopped to help him, but a Samaritan did. The Jews hated the Samaritans because they were "half-breeds." They would never dirty their hands or waste time helping one of them; yet this Samaritan showed compassion on one he knew hated him. At the end of the parable Jesus asked: "Which of these three do you think was a neighbor to the man who fell into the hands of robbers?" There was nothing to say other than, "The one who had mercy on him" (Luke 10:25-37). Compassion for the other person is the outward manifestation of a loving heart.

CHRIST-LIKE LOVE

Many people in the world, when they hear the word compassion, think of someone like Mother Teresa. Born in 1910 in Yugoslavia, she became a nun, serving in India. In 1948, she came across a half-dead woman lying in front of a Calcutta hospital. Mother Teresa stayed with this desperately ill woman until she died. That incident caused her to dedicate the majority of her life to helping the poorest of the poor in India. She became known as the "Saint of the Gutters." She founded an Order with only twelve sisters who were called to serve the poor. Fifty years later, the Order has grown to more than three thousand, serving in one hundred countries worldwide. Mother Teresa saw Jesus in everyone she met, whether they were dying of AIDS or leprosy. She wanted them to die in peace with dignity. For her service to the poor of the world, Mother Teresa won the Nobel Peace Prize in 1979.

God has not called all of us to the kind of compassion Mother Teresa had. But He has called all of us to have compassion for our neighbors, the people we live around, work with, and above all, those we live with. Opportunities often arise where we can show practical compassion that will glorify God. Let me provide an example that occurred during one of my typical days.

PENNIES FROM HEAVEN

For years I have enjoyed walking to help me keep in good physical condition. It provides opportunity to pray, a great avenue for stress release and contributes to good physical health.

But I've developed a rather peculiar habit while I walk. My children tease me about it. I always look for pennies when I walk. It isn't an obsession – at least not yet! I tell my family funny stories that have resulted from me not watching carefully where I am going. I almost hit a telephone pole, had to hurry to get out of the road when I spotted several pennies, and I always make a big scene in the mall when I spot a penny. Strange, huh?

One day Marlene, my youngest daughter Kara, and I took the grandchildren on a trolley ride to downtown San Diego. It was great fun. I had been teasing Kara all day about not finding a penny.

When we returned to our town and were walking toward our car in the parking lot, I put my arm around Kara and told her that there was still hope to find a penny. I looked down, and, behold, I saw a neat packet of cash lying in the parking lot. Wow! It was over a hundred dollars. I went to the Trolley Security office and reported that I had found a large sum of money and gave him my home phone number. He asked how much! Right! I said I would ask that same question to the person who calls.

That night a lady called and left several messages at home. When I called her it seemed she was legitimate. There was no purse, no identification or anything else that she could use to demonstrate that the money was truly hers. After being convinced it was hers I agreed to bring it to their home.

I wasn't familiar with that area of town and so had her teenage son meet me at a nearby store. I stood in the parking lot with over a hundred dollars cash in my hand. I told him I'd give him the money—but I wanted to tell him a very important story first. I had the absolute joy of presenting the gospel of Christ to him. I gave him some materials and booklets that I'd written.

When we got home his mom called and said she found it hard to believe that someone would try to find the person who lost cash money. I told her why it was important for us to make every effort to find her. I asked if we could come to her home to talk to her about God's great love. She was spontaneous and enthusiastic. Marlene got a lovely food basket and gift for the family. They were thrilled with the expression of our love.

When we got there she had invited the neighbor lady over to hear about God. It was clearly a divine appointment. She was on welfare and had taken her last bit of money to help her brother get out of jail for the holidays. She did not know she lost her money until she got home.

Now before you begin to see a small halo forming over my head, let me be quick to say that the hero of the story is God the Holy Spirit. It is true that one of the critical ingredients in our portrait in progress is a sensitive compassion. We were able to express love to others because the Master Artist has begun the work of re-creating us into His glorious image. His great love shining through us!

COMMON DENOMINATOR: SELFLESSNESS

◆

**Courage, confidence, and compassion are all
expressions of supernatural selflessness.
These spiritual virtues will grow best in an environment of
selflessness, and frees us up to trust God, love others, and deny self.**

◆

It sounds like an exercise in confusion to talk about self-esteem and selflessness. Wasn't feeling self-less the very thing that triggered this whole idea of self-esteem? Not exactly. Stanley C. Baldwin ran into this same problem when he was preparing to speak at a seminar at a church. "'This could confuse some of our people,' a pastor told me, referring to my seminar flyer. 'We have been teaching them for years to renounce self, that the self-life is base and sinful. Now you want to tell them how to "like themselves, free themselves and develop their potential." You should avoid that kind of language because it smacks of humanism and runs counter to the biblical description of man.'" Mr. Baldwin says he felt somewhat intimidated. So he dug out his concordance and followed up on the way the Bible uses the word self. He discovered that it was not expressed in a negative sense but "was mostly used in a morally neutral sense as in the reflexive pronouns (myself, himself, yourself)."23 He goes on to say that if you have been taught that self is bad, you have been mis-taught.

So, then, what do we mean by "selflessness"? There are two opposing ways in which people can love themselves: selflessly and selfishly. Selflessly is self-preserving; selfishly is self-destroying. Self-acceptance and selflessness are interrelated. Self-acceptance excludes self-centeredness. Self-love used in the biblical sense of self-acceptance is the exact opposite of narcissism. Self-love makes selflessness possible. Selflessness means that:
• You are free from yourself.

99

- You are more concerned about others' needs than your own.
- You are more concerned about giving than receiving.

The relationship between self-love and selflessness is described in 1 Corinthians 13:5: "Love is not self-seeking." The life of Christ best exemplifies a selfless life. Even though he was the Son of the Most High God, He left His heavenly home to come to earth to live and die for us.

PROGRESS CHECK

Here are some thoughts that can help you see how well you are progressing. Experts agree that there are basically three essential components in a healthy self-image: (1) a sense of belonging; (2) a sense of worth; (3) a sense of competence.

A sense of belonging means that you feel accepted or acceptable. You feel warm, comforted, loved, wanted, just as you are, unconditionally. You will be missed when you are absent.

A sense of worth and value means that you count. You have something to offer. Your perceptions, thoughts, and opinions are important or are significant. You are worthy of respect; you are equal to others.

A sense of competence means that you can do this task, can cope with this situation and are able to meet and handle life's difficulties well. You are an able person in general. You make good decisions. You are achieving and being affirmed as a person of good judgment.

These factors may not last if they come only from your own exertion; but if they come from a harmony of your efforts and God's leading, you can be assured of a biblically sound and personally satisfying self-perception.

When our portrait is being completed with the help of the Master Artist, it will reflect the image of Christ. The world will know we are Christians by our love. "Therefore, as God's chosen people, holy and dearly loved, clothe yourselves with compassion, kindness, humility, gentleness and patience. And over all these virtues put on love, which binds them all together in perfect unity" (Colossians 3:12, 14).

DON'T QUIT

The folklore surrounding Poland 's famous concert pianist and prime minister, Ignace Paderewski, includes this story: A mother, wishing to encourage her young son's progress at the piano, bought tickets for a Paderewski performance. When the night arrived, they found their seats near the front of the concert hall and eyed the majestic Steinway waiting on stage. Soon the mother found a friend to talk to, and the boy slipped away. When eight o'clock arrived, the spotlights came on, the audience quieted, and only then did they notice the boy up on the bench, innocently picking out "Twinkle, Twinkle, Little Star."

His mother gasped, but before she could retrieve her son, the master appeared on the stage and quickly moved to the keyboard. "Don't quit – keep playing," he whispered to the boy. Leaning over, Paderewski reached down with his left hand and began filling in a bass part. Soon his right arm reached around the other side, encircling the child, to add a running obbligato. Together, the old master and the young novice held the crowd mesmerized. [24]

In our lives, as incompetent and incomplete as we may sometimes feel, it is the Master who surrounds us with confidence, courage and compassion. And when the challenges of life become overwhelming and we cannot see His glory in our incomplete image – He whispers in our ear, "Don't quit – don't quit – keep on painting and I will see that the portrait is complete with amazing beauty.

PERSONAL EVALUATION
&
PRACTICAL APPLICATION

God knows what He is doing. Our job is to determine to cooperate and let Him complete our portraits. This is what I call the Divine-Human Cooperative. Cooperating with God is difficult for us. We drift back and forth into the picture of ourselves, letting self-conscious insecurity blemish the confident portrait He is painting. One of the results of our distorted image is our difficulty in trusting God. Day by day we can strengthen that trust in Him by several practical means.

1. Memorize Scriptures that show how God pictures you. The Bible says God made you (Psalm 139:13-16), God loves you (Ephesians 2:4-5), God accepts you (John 1:12), God cares for you (I Peter 5:7), and God has a plan for your life (Ephesians 2:10).

2. Talk to the Master Artist and reaffirm daily your commitment to allow Him to change you into His glorious likeness.

3. Find a godly confidant you can share your commitment with, one who will hold you accountable.

4. Interview someone you know who (like the Emerts) have demonstrated a strong confidence in God. Ask what they attribute their growth in faith to.

5. List several life issues you are now facing that require faith-stretching confidence. List several life experiences that best depict how faith, hope, and love are being painted into your life portrait.

8

THE SHOWING

Critiquing Your Self-Portrait

The artist stood by her self-portrait and nervously watched as the doors to the gallery opened and people began to enter. The professor had hired space in a local gallery for all the students to display their works. He stood at the door and welcomed the visitors, directing them to different parts of the gallery and the various artists. *This is where the rubber meets the road, or should I say, where the paint meets the canvas,* the artist thought to herself. It would be not only a critiquing of the various art works, but also a critiquing of the professor.

She tried to control her trembling, forced a big smile on her face, and watched as the first of the crowds came toward her. "Oh, a self portrait. It looks just like you."

"Now that's what I call real art; you can tell what it is right away."

"My word, what a lovely girl. There is so much joy and life in her portrait."

The artist beamed and accepted the compliments. She knew in her heart that she would have to remind herself every day for awhile what kind of a person she had been transformed into. She would have to go over all the lessons she had learned, confirm the teaching she had heard, believe that she was a true product of the professor.

When an immigrant comes before the immigration court to be sworn in as a new citizen of the United States, he or she repeats this oath: " I hereby declare, on oath, that I absolutely and entirely renounce and abjure all allegiance and fidelity to any foreign prince, potentate, state or sovereignty, to whom or which I have heretofore been a subject or citizen; that I will support and defend the Constitution and laws of the United States of America against all enemies, foreign and domestic; that I will bear true faith and allegiance to the same; that I will bear arms on behalf of the United States when required by the law; that I will perform noncombatant service in the armed forces of the United States when required by the law; that I will perform work of national importance under civilian direction when required by the law; and that I take this obligation freely without any mental reservation or purpose of evasion; so help me God."

Did you know that we have a kind of oath of allegiance as immigrated citizens of the Kingdom of God? Peter tells us what it is: "But you are a chosen people, a royal priesthood, a holy nation, a people belonging to God, that you may declare the praises of him who called you out of darkness into his wonderful light. Once you were not a people, but now you are the people of God; once you had not received mercy, but now you have received mercy. (1 Peter 2:9-14).

What does this have to do with critiquing your portrait in progress? You'll have to check yourself out every once in a while to see how you're doing in becoming more like Christ. You can become more self-assured when you realize who you are in Christ:
• You Have a New Citizenship.
• You Have a New Nature.

- You Have Access to God and to His Great Love.
- You Are Fully Protected by God.
- You Have a Glorious Inheritance.

What a wonderful spiritual example this is to follow! You're a child of God Almighty. There is no better position in all the universe. Let's look at each of these "you haves" and "you ares."

YOU HAVE A NEW CITIZENSHIP

We were originally created in the image of God. Before the fall into sin we were beautiful. Our countenance reflected the attributes of the Creator. The term for "countenance" in Hebrew means "image-bearer." However, our image was tarnished and blemished as a result of sin. Our perfect image was lost.

Those who commit their lives to Christ begin the lifetime process of being re-created to the original image of God. You become a Portrait in Progress.

Our Heavenly Father looks at us, sees through our sin into our heart, and declares us beautiful in His sight. He loves us so much that he sent his only Son, Jesus Christ to die on Calvary's cross so we could receive his gracious forgiveness. He did not send Jesus to condemn us but so that, through His sacrifice and full payment for our sins, we could be fully forgiven–fully restored to His perfect image.

The first step to placing yourself on the easel of the Master Artist is to ask God to forgive your sins in the name of Jesus Christ who paid the penalty for all our sins. God will forgive you of your sins and will cleanse you from all the ugly scars of unrighteousness. Ask him to come into your heart and to forgive you of your sins and be your Lord and Savior. Then, just watch as He fashions you into His glorious image. Little by little, you will take on the countenance of Christ in character and spiritual living.

Today can be the day you let God begin to change you! Someday you will look at the "before" and "after" portraits on the mantel of your imagination. You will see that you no longer look like the first picture because the Master Artist has been changing you more and more into the image of your Creator. Genesis says that in the beginning God created man in His own image. If we let Him, He will continue to paint our portraits in His image, until they become the masterpieces He envisions. Just imagine what the final picture will be like at the end of time, when we see Him face to face, image to image.

If you are a born-again Christian you have a new citizenship. Your immigration into the "better country—a heavenly one" (Hebrews 11:16) was foretold by Hosea: "I will show my love to the one I called 'Not my loved one.' I will say to those called 'Not my people,' 'You are my people'; and they will say, 'You are my God'" (Hosea 2:23). Peter picked up on this in his first epistle: "Once you were not a people, but now you are the people of God; once you had not received mercy, but now you have received mercy" (1 Peter 2:10). When you can see yourself as a person created by the Master Artist, you begin to realize that you are a person of God, a citizen in His kingdom. What a tremendous boost to your self-esteem!

YOU HAVE A NEW NATURE

"Praise be to the God and Father of our Lord Jesus Christ, who has blessed us in the heavenly realms with every spiritual blessing in Christ. For he chose us in him before the creation of the world to be holy and blameless in his sight. In love he predestined us to be adopted as his sons through Jesus Christ, in accordance with his pleasure and will" (Ephesians 1:3-5).

"Christ died for all, that those who live should no longer live for themselves but for him who died for them and was raised again. Therefore, if anyone is in Christ, he is a new creation; the old has gone, the new has come!" (2 Corinthians 5:15, 17).

When a young couple adopted an orphaned baby boy from one of the eastern European countries they soon discovered that the child suffered from "attachment disorder." For months after his adoption as an infant, the child would not allow himself to be hugged, cuddled, or touched. Some of the symptoms of this condition are: inability to give and receive affection in a real way; lack of eye contact; indiscriminate affection with strangers; marked control problems; extreme defiance and anger; destructiveness. It seemed to take a long time before the child began to respond to the deep love of his adopted parents. But by the time he was five years old he had submitted to his loving, caring environment; he became a child with a new nature.

James tells us that we too must submit to love and receive the new nature: "Submit yourselves, then, to God, come near to God and he will come near to you" (James 4:7).

YOU HAVE ACCESS TO GOD'S GREAT LOVE

"At that time [while you were yet an unbeliever] you were separate from Christ, excluded from citizenship, without hope and without God in the world. But now in Christ Jesus you who once were far off have been brought near through the blood of Christ. For through him we both have access to the Father by one Spirit (Ephesians 2:12-13, 18).

David is a wonderful example of a person who knew he had access to God. The book of Hebrews explains that the Old Testament saints received the promise of a Savior by faith, even though they never lived to see the Son of God come to die for them. So David always called on God for all his needs and to voice his complaints. Listen to his Psalm 23: "The Lord is my shepherd, I shall lack nothing. He makes me lie down in green pastures, he leads me beside quiet waters, he restores my soul. He guides me in paths of righteousness for his name's sake. Even though I walk through the valley of the shadow of death, I will fear no evil, for you are with me; your rod and your staff, they comfort me. You prepare a table before me in the presence of my enemies. You anoint my head with oil; my cup overflows. Surely goodness and love will follow me all the days of my life, and I will dwell in the house of the Lord forever." The same God who provided for David will provide for you. Through Christ you have access to the Master Artist. He will hear your prayer and answer to your greatest benefit.

YOU ARE FULLY PROTECTED BY GOD

Not only will God provide for you and protect you from enemies here on earth, even in heaven He continues to defend you from the wiles of the Evil One; just as He did in Job's day.

The book of Job describes how Satan joined the "rest of God's angels to present themselves before the Lord. The Lord said to Satan, 'Where have you come from?' Satan answered the Lord, 'From roaming through the earth and going back and forth in it'" (Job 1:6-8). He was looking for candidates for his kingdom, those he could win away from God. He is still at work. Satan continues to prowl "around like a roaring lion looking for someone to devour" (1 Peter 5:8).

Jesus Christ, God's Son, our Advocate, sits at God's right hand, pleading our case before the Father whenever the Evil One tries to bring evidence against us. "My dear children I write this to you so that you will not sin. But if anybody does sin, we have one who speaks to the Father in our defense, Jesus Christ, the Righteous One. He is the atoning sacrifice for our sins" (1 John 2:1-2). "Therefore he is able to save completely those who come to God through him, because he always lives to intercede" for you (Hebrews 7:25).

YOU HAVE A GLORIOUS INHERITANCE

"Those who are led by the Spirit of God are sons of God. For you did not receive a spirit that makes you a slave again to fear, but you received the Spirit of sonship. And by him we cry, 'Abba, Father.' The Spirit himself testifies with our spirit that we are God's children. Now if we are children, then we are heirs, heirs of God and co-heirs with Christ'" (Romans 8:12, 14-15).

The Duke of Norfolk once sent the priceless Portland Vase to the king of England as an expression of his esteem. The king placed the vase in the British Museum for all to enjoy. Back at the duke's home, a servant was dismissed when it was revealed that he was plotting to overthrow the Duke. Livid with anger and hatred, the servant vowed to get his revenge. He packed up and made his way to London to the British Museum. He watched carefully as visitors filed by the priceless vase. When there were no visitors in the area, and the attendants were out of sight, the servant grasped the beautiful masterpiece, raised it above his head and smashed it to the floor.

Attendants rushed to the scene, but it was too late. The Portland Vase was smashed into a thousand pieces.

When the king heard the news he was both shocked and grieved, but he commanded, "Save every piece. This is my most precious and treasured gift. We'll search for a man who can repair it, no matter what it costs."

It took a long time to find someone whose skills were worthy of the task; he turned out to be a distant relative of the original creator of the vase.25 He came to London and, piece by tiny piece, he restored the vase so that only tiny scars can be seen that attest to its repair. It was placed back in the museum where it can be seen today.

RESTORED

The Master Artist, your Creator God, also sent a relative, His only begotten Son, to restore your brokenness to the original glory of His creation. Only tiny scars can be seen that attest to your repair. Scars made more precious because of the scars the Son of God bore when the Evil One tried to destroy Him on the cross where He gave His life so your life could be fully restored from the damage of sin.

◆

"For God so loved the world that he gave his one and only Son, that whosoever believes in him shall not perish but have eternal life."
John 3:16

◆

PERSONAL EVALUATION
&
PRACTICAL APPLICATION

If you are a believer, the Master's hand is preparing the final portrait of how you really look: in the image of the Lord Jesus. Meditate on these Bible truths from the *New Living Translation* (NLT); *The Living Bible* (TLB); and the *New International Version* (NIV).

- **I Am His Child.** Romans 8:29 (NLT): "For God knew his people in advance, and he chose them to become like his Son, so that his Son would be the firstborn, with many brothers and sisters."

- **I Am His Choice.** 1 Corinthians 1:25-31 (NIV): "For the foolishness of God is wiser than man's wisdom, and the weakness of God is stronger than man's strength. Brothers, think of what you were when you were called. Not many of you were wise by human standards; not many were influential; not many were of noble birth. But God chose the foolish things of the world to shame the wise; God chose the weak things of the world to shame the strong. He chose the lowly things of this world and the despised things and the things that are not to nullify the things that are, so that no one may boast before him. It is because of him that you are in Christ Jesus, who has become for us wisdom from God – that is, our righteousness, holiness and redemption. Therefore, as it is written: 'Let him who boasts boast in the Lord.'"

- **I Am Renewed by God.** Colossians 3:10 (NLT): "In its place you have clothed yourselves with a brand new nature that is continually being renewed as you learn more and more about Christ, who created this new nature within you."

- **I Am an Inheritor of Eternal Life and His Riches.** 1 Peter 1:3-5 (NLT): "All honor to the God and Father of our Lord Jesus Christ, for it is by his boundless mercy that God has given us the privilege of being born again. Now we live with a wonderful expectation because Jesus Christ rose again from the dead. For God has reserved a priceless inheritance for his children. It is kept in heaven for you, pure and undefiled, beyond the reach of change and decay. And God, in his mighty power, will protect you until you receive this salvation, because you are trusting him. It will be revealed on the last day for all to see."

- **I Am a Receiver of His Spirit.** Galatians 2:20 (NLT): "I myself no longer live, but Christ lives in me. So I live my life in this earthly body by trusting in the Son of God, who loved me and gave himself for me."

- **I am Being Renewed Every Day.** 2 Corinthians 4:15-18 (NLT): "All of these things are for your benefit. And as God's grace brings more and more people to Christ, there will be great thanksgiving, and God will receive more and more glory. That is why we never give up. Though our bodies are dying, our spirits are being renewed every day. For our present troubles are quite small and won't last very long. Yet they produce for us an immeasurably great glory that will last forever! So we don't look at the troubles we can see right now; rather, we look forward to what we have not yet seen. For the troubles we see will soon be over, but the joys to come will last forever."

- **I Am Loved and Favored by God.** Ephesians 2:4-5 (NLT): "But God is so rich in mercy, and he loved us so very much, that even while we were dead because of our sins, he gave us life when he raised Christ from the dead. It is only by God's special favor that you have been saved!"

- **I Am a Receiver of Eternal Joy.** 2 Corinthians 4:18 (NLT): "So we don't look at the troubles we can see right now, rather, we look forward to what we have not yet seen. For the troubles we see will soon be over, but the joys to come will last forever."

- **God Loves Me.** Ephesians 2:4-5 (NLT): "But God is so rich in mercy, and he loved us so very much, that even while we were dead because of our sins, he gave us life when he raised Christ from the dead.

- **God Saved Me.** Titus 3:4-5 (NLT): "But then God our Savior showed us his kindness and love. He saved us, not because of the good things we did, but because of his mercy. He washed away our sins and gave us a new life through the Holy Spirit."

- **God Secures My Salvation.** John 10:27-30 (NLT): "My sheep recognize my voice; I know them, and they follow me. I give them eternal life, and they will never perish. No one will snatch them away from me, for my Father has given them to me, and he is more powerful than anyone else. So no one can take them from me. The Father and I are one."

- **God Has Forgiven Me.** Psalm 103:12 (NLT): "He has removed our rebellious acts as far away from us as the east is from the west."

- **God Accepts Me.** John 1:12 (NLT): "But to all who believed him and accepted him, he gave the right to become children of God."

- **God Has Made Me Secure.** John 6:37 (NLT): "However, those the Father has given me will come to me, and I will never reject them."

- **God Made Me.** Psalm 139:14 (NIV): "I praise you because I am fearfully and wonderfully made."

- **God Has a Different** Way of Seeing Me. 1 Samuel 16:7 (TLB):

"But the Lord said to Samuel, 'Don't judge by a man's face or height...I don't make decisions the way you do! Men judge by outward appearance, but I look at a man's thoughts and intentions.'"

1 John 3:2 (NIV): "Dear friends, now we are children of God, and what we will be has not yet been made known. But we know that when he appears, we shall be like him, for we shall see him as he is."

THE DIVINE PORTRAIT

"Love is very patient and kind, never jealous or envious, never boastful or proud, never haughty or selfish or rude. Love does not demand its own way. It is not irritable or touchy. It does not hold grudges and will hardly even notice when others do it wrong. It is never glad about injustice, but rejoices whenever truth wins out.

We can see and understand only a little about God now, as if we were peering at his reflection in a poor mirror; but someday we are going to see him in his completeness, face-to-face. Now all that I know is hazy and blurred, but then I will see everything clearly, just as clearly as God sees into my heart right now. There are three things that remain: faith, hope and love and the greatest of these is love" (1 Corinthians 13:4-7; 12-13, TLB).

I mentioned earlier a bumper sticker that read: "It's all about me!" The truth of a spiritual portrait in progress is that it becomes less and less about me and more and more about God. It is my prayer that you will experience the liberation and exhilaration of cooperating with the Master Artist as He fashions you into His own likeness. We are truly His workmanship and trophies of His grace.

Trophies of Grace

Ephesians 2:4-10
by Robert Newton

The canvas is
stretched across
the frail frame

The Easel set up
and ready
for the Creator

The paints are
Spirit filled–
love, truth, forgiveness, kindness

The Master raises
His Brush –
His only Brush
Humble and willing
in His hand

Dipped in grace,
He paints
a perfect portrait

A portrait of
a life
renewed by the gift

It is you,
It is me,
trophies of grace

Trophies of grace
upon display
for all to see.

Bibliography

1 Joel Hemphill, *"He's Still Workin' on Me."* Copyright 1980 by Hemphill Music Company and Family and Friends Music.

2 Max E. Anders, *30 Days To Understand The Christian Life* (Brentwood, TN: Wolgemuth & Hyatt Publishers, Inc. 1990) p. 349-50

3 "Making the Connection," *The Artist's Magazine,* April 1998, p. 18.

4 W. Hugh Missildine, M.D., *Your Inner Child of the Past* (New York: Pocket Books, Simon & Shuster, Inc., 1963), pp. 32-34.

5 Lloyd H. Ahlem, *Do I Have to Be Me?* (Ventura, CA: Regal Books, 1973), pp. 53-54.

6 W.E. Vine, *Expository Dictionary of New Testament Words* (Grand Rapids, MI: Fleming H. Revell Company, 1959), p. 194.

7 John Ortberg, *The Life You've Always Wanted* (Grand Rapids, MI: Zondervan, 1997), p. 123.

8 Charles R. Gerber, *Christ-Centered Self-Esteem* (Joplin, MO: College Press Publishing Co., 1996), p. 55.

9 V. Raymond Edman, *But God!* (Grand Rapids, MI: Zondervan, 1962), p. 56.

10 Charles R. Gerber, *Christ-Centered Self-Esteem* (Joplin, MO: College Press, 1996), p. 61.

11 Jack W. Hayford, *Taking Hold of Tomorrow* (Ventura, CA: Regal Books, 1989), pp. 144-146).

12 Sabine Baring-Gould, "Onward Christian Soldiers," v. 2.

13 James Dobson, *Emotions: Can You Trust Them?* (Ventura, CA: G/L Publications, 1980), p. 11.

14 William J. Diehm, "Building Self-Esteem," *Today's Christian Woman*, Summer 1983, p. 50.

15 David Augsburger, *Caring Enough to Forgive* (Ventura, CA: Regal Books, 1981), p. 50.

16 Ibid., p. 72.

17 Ibid., p. 91.

18 Steven J. Lawson , (*Men Who Win,* 1992,; Navpress, Colorado Springs, Colorado), p. 156.

19 Max E. Anders, *30 Days to Understanding the Christian Life* (Brentwood, TN: Wolgemuth & Hyatt, Publishers, Inc.,1990), p.175.

20 *AARP Bulletin*, October 1998, p. 23.

21 *Contemporary Illustrations for Preachers, Teachers, and Writers* (Grand Rapids, MI: Baker Books, 1996), p. 111.

22 Bruce Larson, *There's a Lot More to Health Than Not Being Sick* (Waco, TX: Word Books, 1981), p. 26.

23 Stanley C. Baldwin, *A True View of You* (Ventura, CA: Regal Books, 1982), pp. 7-8.

24 "Illustration for Preaching & Teaching," *Leadership Journal,* (Grand Rapids, Michigan: Baker Books, 1993). p. 221.

25 Wolf Mankowitz, *The Portland Vase and the Wedgwood Copies*, (1954).